LOCKDOWN

Life in the tin

Compiled by Harriet Powell

Cover and illustrations by M.R. Goodwin

Copyright © 2020 by Harriet Powell

All rights reserved. No part of this publication may be reproduced, distributed, or transmitted in any form or by any means, including photocopying, recording, or other electronic or mechanical methods, without the prior written permission of the publisher, except in the case of brief quotations embodied in critical reviews and certain other non-commercial uses permitted by copyright law.

Contributors' names have been changed unless otherwise requested.

First Printing 2020

The Little Taboo Press

ISBN 9798680193099

Foreword by Shelter

Shelter is honoured to be supported through this book and welcomes the opportunity for people's experiences of the lockdown to be heard.

Shelter was founded in 1966 to act upon the inequalities and poor provision of housing. Sadly, our services are needed more than ever over 50 years on, not least during the current pandemic. We provide advice, support and guidance to people who are homeless, who are facing homelessness or who are experiencing bad housing, through our telephone and web chat, face-to-face support and range of legal services. We campaign for a future where everyone has a right to a safe home. We are a charity and rely upon support to keep our services and work going. We simply would not be able to do this without our fantastic supporters.

Thank you to Harriet, and to everyone who has made this book a reality during this difficult time.

Lindsay Tilston Jones

Introduction

At the beginning of lockdown, I remember someone saying to me, "Oh well! At least we're all in the same boat."

They couldn't have been more wrong.

This year – this weird, *weird* year – we might all have been sailing on the same sea, but we most certainly haven't been in the same boat. The pandemic has affected us in a multitude of different ways: physically, emotionally, mentally, financially, educationally. Some have had a relatively easy ride. For others it has been devastating.

I hope this collection of personal accounts, all written between March and June 2020, goes some way towards showcasing the range and depth of people's experiences. It is a glimpse into a few of the most intense months in living memory: a snapshot of life in the time of coronavirus.

Helena's story

If I close my eyes I can hear it. The pre-show sounds of the orchestra tuning and singers gently warming up. This is my life.

And now? In the darkness, all I can hear is my heartbeat. But that in itself has become music to my ears.

Overture

I'm an opera singer. It's all I've ever wanted to do. I work around the world, singing high notes for a living and filling opera houses with my voice. I have worked so hard to get to this point and wouldn't have it any other way.

I'm about to fly to Italy to star in a big show…but the night before I leave, a haunting melody interrupts my sleep. It is Covid-19, all set to take over the world and shut everything down, including our theatres.

And then there is nothing. Not even a melody. Just silence and uncertainty. Stay home. Just breathe.

Act 1: Covid-19

Try to work from home.
Wear a mask.
Don't wear a mask.
You can still fly.
Don't fly.

Conflict, confusion, fear – and then frustration. Only my dog is happy. He looks at me smugly as I sit by my piano with the lid shut, staring aimlessly into the distance. He puts his paw on my lap to offer some sort of sympathy. A sign of what is to come.

It starts with a dry cough. My husband raises his eyebrows and moves to the other end of the sofa. By the morning my temperature has soared above 39 degrees.

I have all the symptoms, and so I call the helpline.

Just stay home, Ma'am.

I soldier through the sweats. Fatigue hangs over me. I can barely make it out of bed. My body feels heavy. I seem to have lost all of my senses. All I can do is sleep. I don't even have the energy to dream.

I ask the universe to make it stop, but the universe is busy.

After twelve long days I start to feel like I can face the world again, so I take my dog out for a little walk.

Something feels wrong, so I call the helpline.

How is your breathing?

I laugh down the phone. Sheesh, these lungs are made of STEEL! Don't you worry about my breathing!

Stay home, Ma'am.

Just breathe.

Act 2: The Emergency Room

The next morning everything seems OK. I go downstairs and make some tea. All of a sudden I gasp.

I can't breathe.

WHY CAN'T I BREATHE?

I open the back door to get some air. Everything is spinning. I try to call out to my husband, but the little air I have left is busy keeping me alive.

Cold fear creeps over me.

Breathe, Helena, just breathe. You've got this.

But, I haven't 'got this'.

I call the ambulance.

I text my husband: EMERGENCY.

As I'm lifted into the ambulance, all I can see is his little face, frozen in terror. I want to call out to him, but for the first time in my life I have no voice.

Now I'm in the Emergency Room. Thousands of questions, swabs, needles, scans, doctors in masks with no smiles, white lights, endless amounts of oxygen being pumped down my throat. This goes on for hours and then finally I am taken to my confined room. A bed, four walls and medical equipment.

That's it.

No personal items, no visitors, no colour.

When do I get answers?

I can't get up unassisted. I can't breathe without the oxygen mask. I'm scared, vulnerable and alone, with nothing for company but the sound of my hospital monitor beeping at me.

In the morning I'm told I have the largest blood clot on my lungs the doctors have ever seen. They are surprised I am alive. I'm convinced it's because I know how to breathe.

Days roll into nights. I have more tests than I care to count. Every day my blood is taken. There are more swabs. More needles. An infection develops from the clot. It settles on the lower left side of my lung. Every time I take a breath, there is a sharp pain. Every time I take a breath, I think it could be my last. Painkillers, antibiotics by drip, bruises covering my arms and stomach from the double injections every day. I'm quite a work of art.

It may sound odd, but I'm so proud of my lungs. Stuff you, Covid! Stuff you, Lung Clot! This ain't my time! I've been fighting the impossible all my life.

I give myself small goals each day. Can I walk to the wall without my oxygen levels dropping? Can I sing a few notes?

Just try stopping me...

Act 3: Home

Finally I'm ready to go home. For the first time in ten days I feel the sunshine on my face. Bliss.

It takes time to adjust. My husband treats me like a sheet of crystal, worried he might shatter me.

Four days later, I sit at the piano. Hello old friend. It's me. I try a few gentle scales, but I can barely manage to sing a bar. I feel exhausted. I can hardly move. I cry.

The next day I try again, with more determination. I'm exhausted, but this time I refuse to break down.

And now? Recovery is slow, but I know I'm going to get there. I sang a full piece the other day. Four glorious bars without a breath. I did it. It almost felt like 'normal'. I cried. But for all the right reasons.

Just breathe?

Yup.

Cue the music.

I'm back.

John's story

8th May 2020: at least, that's what the calendar tells me. It's not really relevant now. Every day is Groundhog Day – and let me tell you, it's nowhere near as funny as the movie.

Life in a small Spanish village bordering the Mediterranean Sea sounds (and often is) idyllic. From Easter until October the whole area is busy with tourists, and the streets, shops, restaurants and beaches are packed with folk enjoying their holidays. It's a well-established routine and one that the village and its inhabitants rely upon for a living.

Or they did until Covid-19 arrived. The resulting lockdown has turned everybody's worlds upside-down and inside-out. The only thing missing is Clint Eastwood riding in on his horse down the main street...

One of the biggest problems is that you have a lot of time to kill. The fact that you live in a stunningly beautiful place is about as much use as an ashtray on a motorbike when you consider that you can't go out and take advantage of that beauty.

Only one person per household is allowed out to buy supplies from the local supermarket. No travel outside the village is permitted and you are fined if you try it on. At the supermarket PPE is handed out, everyone is kept at a safe distance from each other and receipts are checked by the local police to ensure people aren't just looking for an excuse to leave the house. Surreal!

Of course, not everybody follows the rules. There are people walking down the road with 'shopping' – in most cases a five-day-old loaf of bread and a couple of carrots – to justify them being out and about. Dogs are rented out to neighbours so they can go for a walk – the neighbours, that is! And cars are being pulled over, only for the police to discover that people are trying to sneak away on holiday with their children and dogs in the boot. WHY? The beaches are closed, and no businesses are open. On the plus side, we have managed to finish watching Netflix in its entirety and I have been getting up earlier than usual to ensure I'm not too late for the sofa. We also have a holiday planned in Puerto Backyarda. My hair is longer than it's been for thirty years and my wife says I should try out for the new series of *Worzel Gummidge*.

Of course, the longer the lockdown goes on, the more time you get to reflect on how life has altered. Things that we all take for granted have probably changed forever. I have come to realise that human contact is vital and that more people should make an effort to be considerate when this is over. There's never been a better time to start.

My two boys live and work in the UK, as there's so little employment over here. I worry about them staying safe and healthy. Just because they're adults doesn't stop them being 'my boys'. The eldest and his partner have just become parents for the first time, and although we're over-the-moon for all three of them, we're also filled with sadness that it may well be months before we get to hold our first grandchild. Video calls are going to be the norm for the foreseeable future, as no international travel is allowed and the flights we had booked have been cancelled.

I've realised that my wife is the most special thing in my life and also my best friend. It's a good job she loves me so much: there aren't many people who would put up with me.

What will happen if the easing of restrictions results in Covid-19 affecting our village? The average age here is at least 50. And what will the long-term effects on society be? Everything has changed irrevocably. There is no option but to adapt to the new normal – and the longer people continue to be selfish and break the rules, the longer that will take to achieve…

Kate's story

Spring was beckoning, the holidays were approaching, and it would soon be the Summer Term, when I'd make the most of my time with our two-year-old before she started nursery. Our not-quite-newborn was doing his best to keep us in a state of bleary-eyed exhaustion, and things were hectic, as they are with four small children – but life, punctuated as it was by term times, school holidays and domestic routines, was relatively predictable.

Our eldest daughter turned eight the day the schools shut down. That week, as the news changed and the advice shifted, we had already pared back the birthday plans: first by postponing her party; then by cancelling it; and finally by deciding against going out for a pizza on the evening itself (the following day it was announced that all restaurants should close). We would celebrate at home instead.

So I went to the supermarket, and it was then that reality hit: rows of shelves stripped bare; queues snaking round to the back of the shop; an almost tangible sense of panic and fear in the air. And, of course, no loo roll (no wrapping paper, either – perhaps the nation was resorting to wiping its collective bum with the stuff).

Once home, I turned on the news. Schools would be closing in a couple of days. At first, I felt pretty positive. We'd have more time together, and the idea of tutoring our older two girls seemed almost appealing. I'm a fully-trained teacher, after all, and perhaps I could fill in the odd gap in their learning.

Day 1 of home-schooling was joyful. We had received no set work yet. We walked after breakfast, stopping to look at the spring flowers covering the village green. We practised spellings and times tables, read stories, and the six of us had a relaxed lunch together (my husband was no longer commuting into London). In the afternoon the girls painted daffodils. I've got this nailed, I thought.

That night, I checked online for new information. There, on my eldest daughter's school website, was a deluge of tasks. Before long the printer had gone into cardiac arrest and I wasn't far off having one myself. I stayed up so late getting organised, I was too wired to sleep.

Next morning, I was full of hope and determination, but by 9.20 my daughter and I were both in tears. I was consumed with regret: she had pushed against the new 'system' and some harsh words had been exchanged. I yearned to be just 'Mummy' again. And if I did have to be their teacher, then I wanted to be Miss Honey, not Miss Trunchbull.

When you live with multiple small children you often feel like you're being pulled in different directions, but with the added pressures of confinement and home-schooling I had the sensation of being stretched so thinly I might snap. Stress levels rise quickly when the baby's crying, the toddler's whining, the other kids need help with separate lessons and there's a pan on the hob threatening to boil over. I must hear 'Mummy?' a thousand times each day. Some evenings I'm convinced I can hear their little voices calling for me long after they have gone to sleep (isn't this what shellshock's like?).

I longed for more time with our toddler and baby, I was a rubbish teacher and a grumpy mum, and I felt like I was failing at everything. Something had to give.

During a week of pernicious PMT, my husband and I had the mother of all blow-outs. Over the years, he has become a very hands-on dad, but he hadn't realised quite what a circus was going on downstairs each day while he was locked away in his study.

I'd appear at his door for a quick hello on my way to putting the baby down for his morning nap, looking haggard and reporting high levels of frustration all round. By lunch time, he'd find me in an even worse state, finishing off lessons whilst feeding the baby and trying to make sandwiches, surrounded by crap (sometimes literally: we were potty-training). Our toddler, on a good day, might be 'helping' me make lunch (not as sweet as it sounds) or, more often than not, would by now be beside herself with frustration, after yet another morning of me repeatedly telling her to 'wait a minute' while trying to teach. I never stopped and felt totally out of my depth. I needed help.

My husband started to take the pressure off me in small ways when he could, which made a big difference. The key to it all is making sure our toddler gets enough input at the start of the day. Then she'll often play happily while I dart between her, the baby and the morning's lessons.

There are still moments when I want to curl up in a ball under the covers. But, by and large, I think we've all adjusted. I'd even go so far as to say we enjoy home-schooling, though when the little ones are kicking off I feel close to the edge. Our long walks and bike rides following afternoon lessons are blissful (we sacked Joe Wicks early on in favour of these) and our days are now punctuated by happy family meals instead of school pick-ups and drop-offs. I don't miss the school runs, which I have always loathed. And I don't miss carting four kids around for ballet and swimming lessons after school, either. Not one bit.

I am increasingly seeing lockdown as time gained rather than time lost. I love the simplicity it has brought, and hope that this will stay with us, long after coronavirus has packed its bags (that will happen, right?).

I still hate the shopping: the distrustful looks between people as they navigate the crime-scene-taped aisles; the officious types barking at you for taking two steps backwards in a one-way aisle because you forgot the cheddar (if there is any – and you can forget about eggs or flour, which will surely be classed as luxury items after this is over); the overflowing trolley (even at the best of times our average family shop looks like a panic buy). I think of those going without, and of NHS workers finding empty shelves after a gruelling night shift on ICU, and the guilt is huge. I sometimes have anxiety dreams before shopping trips and spend my time in the store trying not to breathe. Despite dousing my trolley handle with disinfectant spray and placing a plastic bag over it, I still feel contaminated. When I get home I have an overwhelming urge to wash and change, and I can't work out whether I feel good or bad about the cupboards being full again.

So, it's a mixed bag for us, this lockdown business. We've all been volatile at times and the bad days can come like a shark from beneath, snapping you up and dragging you under. But we forgive each other. And despite the flare-ups, we've all become so close. I'm much more relaxed about mess (our toddler's latest game involves gathering things from all corners of the house and piling them up in a huge heap. It's a nightmare, but it does keep her quiet while I'm teaching). I've really appreciated the acts of kindness, too: our neighbour making me a birthday cake; the daffodils and Easter eggs dropped off by our local church, even though we're not churchgoers; the farmer who let us feed elder branches to three ecstatic goats on one of our walks.

I wouldn't wish coronavirus on anybody, but I think I'll feel a bit lost once lockdown's over.

Flo's story

It all started on my eighth birthday. School had just finished because of coronavirus and from now on we were going to do lessons at home. It was tricky at first, and my mum still explodes when the technology doesn't work.

My cat loves coronavirus. She is called Cesc and she gets endless amounts of pampers – and sometimes even tuna. I've been able to examine her more closely than usual and I have discovered that she has lots of different poses which she uses to get strokes. She has her 'grumpy' pose and her 'give me strokes now' pose. I know her very well! Cesc is like my shadow because she always follows me.

We have gone on lots of fun walks, too. One of my favourites leads to a golf course where we discovered a house-sized dip that we can run up and down. We call it 'The Hole'! Another of our walks takes us to a windy road called Welders Lane. We have to watch out for cars so we can get out of the way if we need to. At dinner we tell lots of rude jokes. It is a bit (very) chaotic because we laugh so much. Dad joins in because he's working from home and we often eat outside. Meals are a happy time of day. We do lots of things we can't do when we have proper school, like roller-skating and bike rides and playing in the paddling pool at break time.

So coronavirus isn't too bad after all, is it?

Niamh's story

I'm a student at a UK performing arts institution. I had a very intensive start to this academic year, with my two most important college assessments both completed by March. This left the second half of the year quite free, but I was grateful for this, since I had several professional engagements in the spring and summer to prepare for, plus a part-time job.

At the beginning of 2020, I helped out a fellow student who had set a Brecht quotation to music and wanted to do a rough recording. The text was: "In the dark times will there also be singing? Yes, there will also be singing. About the dark times." I remember looking at the score and thinking, "Crikey, that's a bit scary! Are these dark times?" I had no idea how dark things were going to get...

Coronavirus was still a distant rumour when I was involved in a serious accident and put on sick leave. For the first few weeks I was so incapacitated all I could do was lie down and stare at the ceiling. I hardly noticed lockdown starting, though I cheered when the first part of it ended, having spent over four months living a severely restricted lifestyle. There was one silver lining: the spring and summer projects I might have had to cancel were suddenly reorganised for the autumn without me having to lift a finger. I can't say I wasn't relieved!

Before Covid, I had a full schedule: sessions with tutors and coaches; group classes; academic modules; rehearsals and performance projects – adding up to about forty-five contact hours a week. Things have changed out of all recognition. I now receive an hour with my tutor via video, an optional short slot with another tutor, remotely-delivered lectures, a few online talks and a whole-department video call, totalling a maximum of five or six hours.

Staff have done their best, but there has been a lot of student anger at the insistence that we still pay full fees, and I feel especially sorry for international students, who are shelling out big bucks. Some of my friends had been waiting their turn for their starring moment, only to have their performances cancelled without the option of rescheduling, leaving their CVs empty and no-one to witness the fruits of their hard work.

Many students have found it difficult to make progress during lockdown, losing motivation due to despondence, anxiety, loneliness or lack of goals. Others have felt inhibited practising in their homes, lacking the space or privacy to work, fearing ridicule and worried about disturbing key workers. Those with poor internet connection or in different time zones have often missed out on live content. Friends who left the UK before lockdown, thinking they'd be away only a short time, graduated by default without hugging me goodbye.

The yawning chasm of inequality has swallowed even more students than usual. Those not from the 'right' background (ie lacking family support and/or having limited financial means) have found themselves at a huge disadvantage. Although some of them have remained in their local accommodations, many have returned home to their families further afield. I remember looking at the videos of two fellow students side-by-side on a conference call screen: one was living alone in a tiny, low-ceilinged, grotty studio-flat with no piano, recording material on a mobile phone with the neighbours banging on the walls, whilst the other was in a home concert hall, complete with grand piano and professional recording equipment. I pondered how these two were supposed to have the same educational experience without college facilities to level the playing field.

For me, the biggest disappointment was yet to come. I felt an immense pressure to recover quickly and was worried about future opportunities and people finding out about my injury and not employing me. I'm young and physically fit, so I started to exercise, pushing myself a little further every day. In the middle of lockdown, I had to be taken to hospital. The consultant gave me a massive telling-off: apparently I had narrowly avoided requiring emergency surgery. I was so frustrated – my attempts at getting better faster had seriously backfired!

Once I got home I emailed the relevant college staff to tell them the news, but no one replied. I emailed them again the following week, only to receive a message saying they didn't understand why my email warranted a response. The same day I got a reminder that my next fee instalment was due. I felt like college didn't care if I lived or died – as long as I paid my fees.

The term fizzled out towards the end of lockdown with no real certainty about what the next academic year would bring. Some universities and colleges have already committed to next year being online, whilst others are saying they may open in a limited capacity. All around the globe new students are trying to work out whether or not to take up their places and existing students are deciding whether or not to return.

I am one of them.

Tony's story

My year started to go awry last August. On holiday we received a phone call to say that our much beloved cat, Nino, had died.

A few days later I got the news that my mother had died. I packed my things (completely inappropriate for a New Zealand winter) and got on a plane. We said our goodbyes to her in a moving service in a beautiful wooden church on one of the hills in Dunedin.

I spent a very precious month with my sister and father. We talked, ate and reminisced on the good, the bad and the complicated in my mother's life. We drove up the South Island together, admiring the beauty of the landscape and the power of the sea. In the middle of September I returned to my job in Germany, promising myself that I would engage in some counselling to help me make sense of my relationship with my mother. Of course, I had no time for this. I was so busy. It would have to wait.

In January I went back to New Zealand. My father's health had taken a turn for the worse, and he had spent an extended period in hospital with pneumonia. He seemed to have recovered, but soon ended up in hospital again, where he was pampered by the nurses and brought back, once again, to something resembling health.

A place was found for him in a rest home, and it was there that we watched him shrink, evaporate and become more and more translucent. All the while, we propped up the fiction that he was simply getting his strength back in order to return home. My sister and I knew that this was not so. We were at best too charitable and at worst too cowardly to tell him this. He was in terrible pain and would occasionally say, "I think I might be on the way out", which would invariably elicit a placatory response from me. I hated myself for not being honest.

On 19th February he drifted off. I was present, but only sort of. My own inability to believe that my father was dying meant that until moments before, I was busy making phone calls trying to arrange something or other, rather than sitting solemnly by his bedside, waiting with reverence for his soul to depart. Eventually I cottoned on that the end was near. I ran to fetch a nurse – what I hoped to achieve, I'll never know – and when I came back he was quite clearly gone.

On 2nd March we held his funeral in the cathedral in Dunedin. We had a wonderful service, surrounded by many friends, with three very moving eulogies and much fine music. I decided to stay in New Zealand for another three weeks: there was much to do.

All this time – even before I left Germany – I had been hearing snippets, and then increasingly alarming reports, about the coronavirus epidemic in China. It was a bit like a rather vague plotline in a story, occupying more and more space until you realise it is actually what the whole thing was about all along. It had already changed my travel plans, which were to have included some time in China on the way home, though my father's failing health would have altered that anyway.

Things became more and more real. I was due to go home on 19th March but was unsettled by the pictures in the media of thousands of people packed like sardines into planes and airports. I decided to delay for a week, hoping (how naïve) that the huge streams of people moving around the globe would abate a little.

And then everything went quiet. I had missed the boat – or the plane. On 25th March New Zealand went into lockdown, and everything just stopped. There were no cars, no planes, no people. Nothing. We were allowed out for exercise, and I grasped this opportunity to enjoy the outdoors and keep myself sane. I ventured further and further afield, sometimes up to twelve miles a day. Often I walked up the small mountains behind my house: Mount Cargill, Swampy Summit and Flagstaff. I walked to the sea. I walked through almost every suburb of Dunedin. I walked through the centre of town. And everywhere I was greeted by silence. Eventually, of course, the sounds came back – the engines, the hustle and bustle of a small city. But to begin with there was stillness. To be walking along George Street and hear nothing but the sound of one's own feet is eerie: it's not like walking home through a deserted street at 4am after a party. The silence is everywhere. And it's all the time.

I am very fortunate: I had an easy ride. I had somewhere to live, I had enough money, I didn't become an alcoholic or lose my routine. I even started having some counselling.

Now everything has all but gone back to normal. New Zealand has, to date, dodged the bullet. We are at Level 2 and life is returning to the streets. Outside is dominated by the sound of cars and – this is New Zealand – chainsaws. As in so many other places, the repellent maunderings of populist idiots are also figuratively blotting out more pleasant thoughts and sounds. "Nothing happened," they say. "Why did the government curtail our civil liberties?" "Why couldn't I get fast food during the lockdown?"

At the time of writing (mid-May) I am still here, waiting for that magical flight which will take me home to Germany. The chances are good that I will make it by the second week of June. I came to New Zealand for four weeks and will have been here five months. I miss my family terribly: despite frequent phone calls they seem very far away. I spend my days sorting through my parents' effects, alternately delighted and appalled by what I find, holding some arcane object in my hand and wishing I could ask them its history, or even why the hell they didn't throw it out years ago.

I can't, though. They're gone. I have lost both my parents and been separated from my own family for months. I still miss the cat. What, however, will stay with me when I think back on all this is the sound of my feet, walking and walking: a drop in a vast ocean of silence.

Sarah's story

I've just spent thirty minutes performing my daily ritual of pumping water out of the bilge. I don't know where it's coming from. I can't help thinking the scriptwriter of my life has resorted to very obvious simile, using the well-worn metaphor of a slowly-sinking boat to illustrate my slowly-sinking life. The scriptwriter has a lot to answer for and I think her sense of humour is decidedly sadistic. Why am I on this rotten, sinking boat, all alone at the age of 51? How has my life become this?

We decided to buy a boat after a wine-fuelled conversation with friends who'd done it themselves. It seemed like a great idea: adventure; travel; freedom from capricious landlords. We'd finally have our own home. "But I want to do it now," I said to my partner, Nick. "I want to do it while we're young and healthy enough to enjoy it, not wait ten years until we're 60."

These words haunt me, day and night…

We located a 58ft boat, had a survey and bought it, but our first voyage ended abruptly when the engine overheated after about twenty minutes. We moored up, and the first in a long line of canal-boat engineers arrived as if by magic and started to work on the engine. Within a week she was hauled out into a boatyard: her problems were manifold and serious. We got another survey and this one found that her hull was in fact very thin in several places. Extensive welding was needed.

We were worried, we were both holding down freelance careers, and Nick, in particular, was working himself into the ground. Something had to give – and it did. In January 2019 he suffered a subarachnoid haemorrhage and was rushed to hospital. He was operated on and remained seriously ill with a number of horrible complications before being transferred to a rehab unit four months later.

Help came in the unlikely form of his ex-wife. She and my sister offered to get the boat into a reasonable state, so that I could have somewhere to live. A crowdfunding site was set up, and friends and strangers put up a lot of money. I was amazed at people's love and generosity.

Over the summer, Nick gradually came out of his lowered state of consciousness. I'd spend my mornings painting the boat, and my afternoons and evenings doing everything I could to stimulate his brain: singing him songs; doing crazy dancing; reading; playing him music; massaging him with essential oils; stroking his face; loving him; willing him to come back to me. Visiting hours were 2pm-4pm and 6.15pm-8pm, and between 4pm-6.15pm I mainly sat in the car and screamed.

The boat could now be moved and was liveable-in. It wasn't luxurious by any stretch, but at least I had somewhere of my own, albeit leaky and draughty. In February 2020 Nick was transferred to longer-term rehab in Birmingham and I had the boat moved down there so I could be near him. He had his own room, and I could visit at any time of the day or night. Nick and I spent hours and hours together, and we did lots of the things that give him joy. Things were improving.

And then came lockdown.

I hate that word. I hate the sound of it. It's not even proper English. It sounds like something Donald Trump would say: a vacuous neologism.

About a week before the Prime Minister eventually pulled his finger out and declared general shutdown, I had contacted all Nick's family and friends. I'd decided that there should be as few people as possible coming and going from his room. The following week, to my shock and dismay, I found myself excluded, too. And it has been that way ever since.

I have written emails, I have pleaded, I have cried, I have threatened legal action, I have self-isolated in order to pose no threat, hoping that this would sway the powers that be. But all to no avail. The place will not receive visitors.

What's more, I live on a stupid, leaky boat, totally unsuitable for a person with Nick's complicated needs. If I was living in a house or a flat – or anywhere other than this steel white elephant – I would have pressed for Nick to be discharged into my care. But I don't, so I can't. I am as useless to him as – well – a leaky boat. One day I hope we can live together somewhere nice. But not now. It makes me feel desperate, so I try not to think about it too much.

For the first three weeks of lockdown, I obeyed all the rules and stayed inside, biting my nails to the quick and attempting to have contact with Nick via Skype. He found this difficult: I think he views people on a screen quite passively, like they're on TV. I could see that he was going downhill and interacting with me less often, and the staff also said he rarely spoke. I was extremely worried, so when the three weeks were up, I asked if I could visit Nick's window. The manager agreed, so I took some steps to stand on and paid Nick a two-hour visit. This was fairly successful, and he began to speak again.

I have gone to his window every day since, but he has continued to decline. I believe this is because he doesn't get why I am not with him and can't understand what is being said by staff in PPE gear. He has become hard-of-hearing since his illness and needs to see someone's mouth to be able to lipread. His main line of communication is therefore compromised by facemasks, and he has simply stopped bothering to speak.

He has now been in hospital for two weeks because of a non-Covid-related chest infection. We thought his shunts might have become blocked because he recently stopped eating. He has had numerous CT scans, and there's nothing new or worse in his brain pathology. I suspect the reason he isn't eating or communicating is to do with his emotional state.

Nick's understanding is compromised, and his short-term memory is practically non-existent, so he doesn't remember why I'm not with him. I write him a letter most days, and they all say the same thing: you're in quarantine and that's why there are no visitors allowed. But it's difficult to know what he understands.

He will go back to his rehab unit soon and I will resume my daily window visits and keep fighting my battle with the management. I need to see him properly and carry on our work together. There is a balance to be struck between safety against Covid-19 and a loss of regained function, and I think it's gone too far one way already.

Nick is my world, and our time together before his illness was without doubt the happiest period of my life. I want as much of him back as possible.

Until then, I will continue to pump water out of my leaky boat.

Charles' story

I've long been fascinated by chance and the role it plays in all our lives. It's not a particularly fashionable idea. We prefer to believe in cause and effect, in the power of our own agency: we pretend that we're in full control. Listen to any sportsperson being interviewed post-win and they will invariably claim the triumph is the result of their own hard work. Rarely will they consider all the other chance factors that have been in play. They'll never say thank you to their parents for the uniquely beneficial genetic makeup they inherited. And they'll probably overlook the advantages they enjoyed by growing up within spitting distance of outstanding training facilities.

We've all experienced being in the right place at the right time – perhaps a chance meeting with a stranger, which changes life immeasurably for the better. But we also know the dangers of being in the wrong place at the wrong time, when best-laid plans are suddenly upended.

Life is not fair. Yes, we might prefer it to be otherwise, for hardship and wellbeing to be spread more equally across the population, and for the doses of crap and joy to appear at more regular intervals throughout the years so we can prepare and be ready and able when they arrive. But life doesn't work that way. Sometimes the shit-storm happens to those least deserving. And all in one go. And it's tough. It's not your fault. You've done nothing wrong. This wasn't on the job description. Things weren't meant to happen this way. But they have.

For many people – hundreds of thousands, I guess – this has been their experience over recent months: a time of anxiety and uncertainty, tension and loss, sadness and disappointment. But it's not been mine. I'm one of the lucky ones – so far, at least! Because, by chance, I've been in the right place at the right time. It's not because I've been clever or shrewd or because I've isolated better (whatever that might mean). No, on this occasion I've just been lucky.

Without wishing to sound flippant, if Covid-19 had to happen, it has popped into my life at just the right time! If I was twenty years older – in my eighties – I'd probably have a body full of pre-existing health conditions and therefore be the disease's Number One target. I might even be one of those living in a care home, with little chance of getting out again. And if I was twenty years younger? Well, back then, in my forties, I was living in London, with two small children at primary school, a mortgage that would make you weep, a job that I hated, and a bout of depression that a therapist was helping me to cope with. If lockdown had hit me then, I'm pretty sure I would have imploded.

But that was then. This is now. Because of my age and stage of life – 66 years old, children grown up, freelance career – I've spent the last decade living in a remote rural location on the Welsh border, out amongst the sheep and cows. Here, I am as isolated and safe from this sodding disease as anyone can hope to be. I have a lovely house and garden, with a view to die for. I am able to get out and exercise in the local fields and lanes. And the supermarket is happy to deliver wine to my door. I have it very easy. The biggest risk I face is sounding smug.

Of course, there are things I can't do, and my work as a freelance business psychologist has completely dried up. After twenty-two years of building up a successful practice, it has – almost overnight – disappeared. If I allow myself to think about it too much, I can get bloody angry at the injustice and unfairness of it all. The thousands of hours of effort I've put in to develop it, to create something I'm proud of. The risks I've taken. And now it's gone. Indeed, my 'pension' has gone. This wasn't on the plan.

It may not be gone forever, of course. I like to think that when this whole sorry episode is over, my practice – like Lazarus – will rise from the dead. Unfortunately, I know the Bible well enough to remember that Lazarus didn't rejuvenate unaided. Actually, Jesus was around at the time. It was he who performed the miracle, he who helped Lazarus burst back to life. So, unless we have a Second Coming in the next few months, I'm not overly confident of my practice's future. Maybe it has gone forever.

But if that's the case – well, I had an absolute blast for twenty-two years, doing something I loved, working with people I liked, and being paid for it. Will there be a next chapter? Of course there will be. I just don't know what it is yet.

Andrew's story

Cologne, 1st January

I have two goals for 2020: to get my wife pregnant and to run a marathon.

24th January

This morning Lena woke me up, holding two positive pregnancy tests. She is bubbling with joy and I'm so excited. We're about to start the greatest adventure of our lives.

16th February

We visited Lena's grandma to deliver the good news. At first, she was speechless – not the reaction we've come to expect. Before we told her, she had been talking about coronavirus and climate change, asking, "How can people bring children into this dying world?" She eventually got over her initial shock and was happy for us.

26th February

Today we stocked our pantry with canned goods, pasta and other non-perishable food items. In the supermarket we joked about the absurdity of it all, but with coronavirus on Germany's doorstep and a pregnant wife to protect, I felt like we needed to hope for the best and prepare for the worst.

Cologne celebrated 'Karneval' last weekend. Amidst the drunken debauchery, who knows how many people were exposed to the virus? So far, nothing has changed in Germany. People aren't wearing masks. Work hasn't stopped. Events haven't been cancelled. I won't be surprised when quarantine measures are put in place.

3rd March

Lena called me from work, crying. She told me she'd received her blood test results and that her thyroid counts were abnormally high. She was panicking and wanted to go to the gynaecologist to hear our baby's heartbeat. I reassured her, and she eventually calmed down. Little is known about coronavirus, and even less about its effect on pregnant women and unborn babies. Lena is particularly vulnerable due to a chronic blood condition and the lung embolism she suffered five years ago. She and I may need to quarantine for the foreseeable future, so she doesn't contract the virus.

4th March

Today at work I nearly had a panic attack while crammed into a poorly ventilated room with sixty other colleagues. I was aware of every cough, every blown nose, every particle floating through the air hoping to infect me.

9th March

Italy is now in total lockdown. Here in Germany, there are 35 cases in Cologne and two people have died in Nordrhein-Westfalen.

10th March

My half-marathon has been postponed till 18th October. Hopefully, in a few months everything will have settled down a bit and I can sign up for a summer marathon.

15th March

There are now 244 cases in Cologne and Germany is closing its borders.

During my run today I stopped by some volleyball courts to say hello to a friend. We greeted each other with an elbow bump. All the courts were full, with matches in progress. While watching, I couldn't help picturing an enlarged coronavirus molecule in place of the ball as it bounced back and forth over the net.

21st March

There are 773 cases in Cologne and 22,364 in Germany.

On today's walk people were following social-distancing rules, which is a vast improvement on last weekend. We even saw a couple coming out of the supermarket wearing hazmat suits. The playgrounds we passed were taped off and empty. How do you explain that to your children?

31st March

On my bike ride I observed fifteen people getting off a bus. Only two were wearing masks and little effort was made to maintain a safe distance from each other.

1st April

Poor Lena has taken on the role of a Disney princess, trapped in our fourth-floor apartment, let out only for doctor's appointments and daily walks. She depends on me, her gallant prince, to brave the dangers of the supermarket and bring her fresh kiwis.

8th April

There are currently 1,865 cases in Cologne.

While running I try my best to keep my distance from other people, but today, while crossing a bridge, I had to run right past a woman blowing out her cigarette smoke. I covered my face and held my breath. If I come down with coronavirus, that's probably what did it.

24th April

It was a beautiful day for a 15km trail run and so refreshing to run surrounded by nature, without constantly dodging other people. When I got home, Lena was a vision of happiness and beauty, lying on the couch, rubbing her belly. She called me over to come and feel. It was very light, but I felt the tiniest kick.

16th May

Today we went to the baby store. This was our first shopping venture together since the lockdown. We felt safe with our masks on, and it was nice to do such a normal activity.

17th May

During my run through the park, a couple was tossing a football around. The woman's pass went over the guy's head and he walked back to retrieve the ball. As he picked it up, I put my hand out to receive a pass. The ball came floating into my outstretched hands, a perfect spiral. With a smile, I threw it back to the woman. This was the most contact I've had with a non-family member since early March.

4th June

There are currently 38 cases in Cologne. The baby is healthy, Lena is healthy, I am healthy, and we are clinging to each other to get through these strange times, looking towards the light at the end of the tunnel.

Penny's story

When lockdown began and it was announced that our GCSEs were cancelled, my initial reaction was confusion! I don't think my brain actually processed the information for about ten minutes. When I finally got my head around what was happening, my anxiety kicked in and I began to come up with all the worst possible scenarios. What if college didn't take me because my grades weren't up to standard? What if I couldn't get onto the course I wanted? What if I failed half my subjects because I hadn't tried hard enough in my Mocks?

As time went on I managed to keep myself busy and stay entertained. I've learned lots of new life skills, like cooking and cleaning, and my mum jokes that I'll be able to leave home by the time lockdown ends! I also started posting a story on social media every day with a recap of what I'd done, to stop me from sitting around doing nothing. I realised that it could have been much worse: I might have been in the year below, stuck with loads of work to catch up on for next year's GCSEs, or I might have had to attend online classes like my brother. Still, I have to admit it has been tough on my mental health: I was used to seeing my friends all the time, and suddenly I wasn't allowed to see them at all.

Now lockdown has eased, and I can meet up with some of my schoolfriends to go on socially-distanced walks and picnics. We talk about everything that's happened and help each other to come to terms with it, but I really miss being able to hug someone who I haven't spent over three months cooped up in a house with. I think we all just want a bit of normality. The exam dates have now passed, and we didn't actually do any of them…just like that we've finished school, with no prom and no goodbyes.

All I can hope for is that this will soon be over and that my results won't be terrible. I've stopped wasting my time stressing over something that can't be changed and instead I'm using it to prepare myself to face the outside world again and get ready for college – and the future.

Imke's story

I'm a nurse, and recently changed from working in intensive care to surgery: I wanted a break from nights, and time to start my Masters. Life revolved around work, writing essays and sorting out the kids.

Then the email arrived: *You have been identified as having ICU experience. Please contact X to arrange redeployment to ICU with effect from Monday.*

My long-suffering husband has always had to put up with a no-nonsense South African wife, but I don't think he knew what he was getting himself into when he married a nurse, let alone an ICU one. At least he is able to work from home, so there's been no change for him in the past few months.

We have two children, one in Year 9 and the other in Year 6. They are usually busy with sports and clubs, but they say the biggest change for them has not been to do with school, friends or activities but the knowledge that their mum is going back to ICU, where all the Covid patients are.

***

And so…I dig out my multi-coloured pen (ICU nurses will know what I mean) and my calculator and put together a 'Covid bag' which will go from the car to work and nowhere else. It is filled with essentials, and when this is all over it will be binned along with the shoes reserved for ICU. A plastic box is put in my car along with hand sanitiser and wipes for the after-work clean-up operation.

I haven't worked in ICU for two years (and not in my new hospital's ICU at all), so on my first day I feel a mixture of excitement and apprehension. But training and experience quickly kick in and it soon feels as if I never left. The ICU is well-equipped with all the correct PPE – and enough of it to allow staff to go for breaks. The hospital, local groups and various donations of food keep the staff fed and hydrated, and this is greatly appreciated. The white 'boiler suits' are straight out of Hollywood's *CSI* dramas and provide the humour for the day – selfies cry out to be taken and the funny side of a worldwide pandemic laughed at.

The drive home consists of a welfare check on my mother, in isolation three hundred miles north of where I live, and my thoughts then turn to the logistics of how to make it to the shower without touching anything. It goes something like this:

- open the front door

- wipe down the car keys

- strip off in the hall

- streak upstairs to the shower to the sound of shouts from the kids (apparently their mum is 'weird')

By the time I come down, my husband has bundled up my uniform and shoved it into the machine on a hot-wash. The marks on my face from the tight PPE masks are beginning to fade, and I walk into a room full of happy faces. Despite being tired, I realise how lucky I am. I have a comfortable home, a supportive family and a job I love. Yes, even in a pandemic it is nice to be able to go to work and be useful. And in these uncertain times to have a job at all is a huge relief.

***

Throughout all this, we decided to keep the children at home for their schooling. Both schools have been supportive and proactive, and the kids have settled into a routine: our 'new normal'. With a little help from Google, I am still able to do Year 9 Maths and Science, while Music and Martial Arts classes take place via Zoom and Facebook Live. Some lessons have been replaced by more practical pursuits: gardening; painting rooms; cooking; using the sewing machine and Microsoft Office.

We have set aside time for family lunches in the garden, and we're starting to tick off jobs on the DIY list. Time seems to have slowed down, and I don't see that as a bad thing. I sit and stare at the flowers and notice the baby birds in the honeysuckle near the kitchen and the newts in the pond. I talk nonsense with the kids and torture my husband at board games. We re-group as a family. But I still miss things: my hairdresser; coffee with friends; time to myself.

I have chosen to be positive during this pandemic. As nurses we see tragedy on a daily basis, and it is my way of protecting my family and keeping myself sane. You have to be slightly nuts to do the job in the first place! I'm not trying to make light of things, nor play down the global tragedy that is unfolding – it's just my way of coping.

When I look back on this in years to come, my memories of lockdown will not all be bad. I will have had the luxury of time with my family – and that is priceless.

Marie's story

Vienna, 25th February

Just received a text from a Chinese friend living in Munich: *Have you bought masks and filled your kitchen cupboards?* I answer at once: *No! I'm not falling into this hysteria…*

Two hours later, out of curiosity, I look for masks online. All the good ones are sold out. Well, that solves my problem – and anyway, here in Vienna the situation is pretty calm.

***

Fast forward two weeks. Our twelve-year-old daughter, who is an only child, receives information about homeschooling, which will probably begin next week. Everyone must bring their smartphones to school to download apps and practise log-ins. I'm really impressed with how quickly everything is organised, and the calmness and discipline reassure me. With Covid case-numbers going up every day, it's a relief that our daughter will soon stop using the bus and metro and stay at home. She and her friends are excited by the novelty…for the first few days at least.

I decide to put a new routine in place for her immediately. She has ten hours of video calls per week plus homework, all of which gets done in the morning. I finally persuade her to learn the piano with me in the afternoon and we sometimes do fitness videos together. I also introduce her to *Friends*, which she loves! The laughter does us both good and her English really improves.

I try to support our immune systems by making nutrient-dense meals, cutting out sugar and reducing carbs. We go for lots of walks: great for our physical and mental health.

My husband and I are both freelance classical singers and soon find out that seven months' worth of contracts has been cancelled, including a ten-week stint at a big festival in Germany. Our work in Vienna dries up, too. My husband usually sings at a lot of funerals, but only five people are allowed to be present at each one now. His teaching at a music school is moved online. Some of my private teaching also disappears as people's finances dwindle, though I manage to retain three pupils. Our revenue this year will take a massive hit, and any compensation we receive will be small.

We begin to ask ourselves questions:

- why don't the statistics clarify the difference between those who have died with Covid and those who have died from it?

- why are certain recognised experts being censured?

- why not invest in making us all more resilient health-wise, so that we can return to normal life and hug each other again? There are, and always will be, viruses, bacteria and fungi in us, on us and around us.

- should we really be living in a world where masks, social distancing, contact tracing and vaccines are mandatory? Of course, the vulnerable must be protected, but should the elderly be so isolated that they lose the will to live? Should people be allowed to die alone? Should people have treatment, operations and diagnoses postponed, sometimes with dire consequences? Would a more selective lockdown not be more appropriate?

- what about the welfare of our children, deprived of essential social contact with their peers, stuck at home in sometimes difficult family circumstances and having their studies disrupted?

The list could go on and on. Are we going to behave this way every single time a new virus comes along? The repercussions will go on for years.

Perhaps, though, there are positives to be found. The bees are happy. The sky is clear. Perhaps we have been given a chance to protect our planet…and mankind itself.

David and Margaret's story

David

We were virtuous. We had not stockpiled toilet rolls. We were seventy-somethings with underlying health conditions who could readily self-isolate for twelve weeks and exercise self-restraint. We had supplies. The milkman would bring eggs and other dairy products. Our enterprising butcher had spotted an opportunity and would bring potatoes as well as meat.

One week in and the first doubts began to emerge. We spent days trying – and failing – to secure a home-delivery grocery slot. Our chest freezer (bought to support six and now supplying two) was full, but with food for normal times. Menu adjustments would be needed. We would soon run out of essentials. Ice cream would need to be rationed. We would cut down to one coffee a day, but only on weekdays. We were getting anxious…

And then it happened. Like a miracle, a slot appeared. Nervous fingers sped across the iPad, entering provisions – any provisions – to secure our slot. We had two weeks to complete our order and spent those days like children in a sweet shop, feverishly adding everything we might possibly need. This wasn't stockpiling, just forward planning.

The day arrived, and the delivery man came to the door with a grand total of two bags. We were shocked. We'd no idea the nation had already run so short of staple products.

The search for a slot became part of our daily routine. Sitting in a virtual queue at 2am was not a joyous experience, even with Radio 4 for company, but eventually we nabbed another slot and ordered what we could: ie three of nearly everything.

Once again the delivery man brought only two bags. He confirmed that this was our entire order, minus one out-of-stock item.

Panic set in.

We deployed our tactic of last resort and asked one of our children for IT support. A short FaceTime tutorial later, we discovered that the problem lay in our failure to checkout properly. On both occasions, our original order had been recognised, but not our later additions. Our patient son suggested we read the instructions next time.

By chance, we noticed that another supermarket, new to us, was opening a telephone helpline, and at 8am the next morning we rang it. Two hours later a young man answered and listened to our plight. Perhaps he had grandparents, because within minutes he had fixed us up with a delivery time, spotted that we were on the government's over-seventies list and asked if we would like a recurring slot. At last we knew what it must feel like to win the EuroMillions and pledged lifelong loyalty to our new grocer.

This time the delivery man brought eight bulging shopping bags – and then returned with the frozen items. We had triumphed. Unrestrained ice cream consumption could resume.

In the following weeks most purchases went to plan. We could now supply the entire area with cleaning products and razor blades, though the baker of our household was outraged that new entrants to the activity had nabbed all the flour and yeast.

We knew that we had attained true proficiency when we struggled to require enough items to reach the minimum order value. We overcame this with the addition of a bottle of Pimms. But this was special. This was for drinking during our village VE Day virtual street-party. A useful reminder, should it be required, of just how trivial our concerns really were.

Margaret

We began to self-isolate a week before the official lockdown. At least by the end of it all my activities had been cancelled, so I didn't have to make any decisions about whether to go to them or not.

At first it was very stressful. We spent hours on the phone trying to get online shopping and stayed in except for having one walk a day. We had to cancel everything in the diary, including holidays – and we're still trying to get the money back for some of them. At least we managed to celebrate our Ruby Wedding Anniversary just before lockdown.

The worst part is not seeing the children or grandchildren. Online is just not the same. One of them was coming with his family at Easter. Cancelled. Visits to London to see the others? Cancelled, too.

Then there was the adjustment to being at home all the time. I would like to see walls other than our own, and scenery other than just outside the house.

The news is depressing, and I've more-or-less stopped watching it. I don't read the tabloids, and television programmes are mainly repeats.

I know I've lost confidence. I'm assuming that this will come back as normal life resumes. According to a French friend of mine, this feeling isn't uncommon.

One of my sons and his family has had the virus, but they're alright now. We were very worried because we hadn't heard from them for over a week and their WhatsApp replies were somewhat cryptic. When they eventually Face Timed us, my daughter-in-law was quite pale.

I dislike all the false heartiness and the comparisons with the war. And I dislike being told things that I learned as a child presented as something new.

But none of this is unusual. So many people are going through the same thing.

And there are positives…

We are very fortunate. We have a house large enough for us to spend time in different rooms. We have a garden. We don't have to worry about jobs or coping with children in a confined space. We have wonderful neighbours, who get our fruit and vegetables twice a week and collect my prescription. The butcher delivers our meat, and the milkman delivers milk, eggs, bread and orange juice. Several of my activities are now available via Zoom or Face Time.

We talk to our family, who have been very good about keeping in touch. The older grandchildren read out poems they have written, and sometimes we do quizzes. The younger ones say hello and then go off and play while we talk to their parents. Our friends have rung and emailed.

I have been improving my French and Spanish language skills. My husband recently said that he heard me laugh for the first time in weeks when I was speaking to my French friend.

I'm not going to rush to the hairdresser when it reopens. I'm looking forward to discovering the real colour of my hair. I'm not buying any new clothes: I don't need any and

I'm not going anywhere to wear them! I'm not a shopper and never have been, unless it involves meeting a friend and having lots of conversation and coffee!

I have lost track of time completely, although we do differentiate between weekends and weekdays. Wine is for the weekends (except for when it was my husband's birthday). We promised ourselves we'd have no biscuits, cakes or ice cream with our afternoon cup of tea, but we haven't kept this resolution...

When we are allowed out, it's going to be difficult. As my daughter-in-law said, we've become accustomed to this new way of living. It's going to require determination to communicate with actual human beings.

Jessica's story

When we were finally told that school would be closing for the majority of pupils, no one was surprised: over the previous couple of days we'd been frantically preparing home-learning packs to hand out before the students left. Many of the packs ended up having to be hand-delivered as a lot of parents had family members who were self-isolating and were therefore already keeping their children off.

Lessons which could be adapted to be taught at home were drawn up, and in a matter of days we had a new Summer Term curriculum mapped out. School leaders had endless meetings to navigate the legislation and documents that were winging their way daily from the government, the Department for Education and various unions.

Timetables, staffing rotas and classrooms were then reorganised to provide for vulnerable pupils and the children of key workers. Some staff worked from home, preparing lessons that could be accessed by a range of pupils, contacting parents to offer advice and support, and working on curriculum documents for OFSTED (which was canvassing parents to see if they still wanted some form of inspections to take place). They were also, in many cases, home-schooling their own children. For a while, teachers were told how fantastic they were…and then, only a couple of weeks later, how lazy!

We adapted. We met on Zoom, used existing and new online lesson resources, and became a home-delivery service and advice bureau, trying to make sure parents didn't go insane and children didn't go hungry. We worked evenings, weekends and holidays to keep our students educated, motivated, included and – above all – as safe as possible.

And then we re-opened.

We emptied the classrooms, distanced what we could, stocked up on soap and sanitiser, and stored the shareables. We formed safe 'bubbles' of pupils and staff, who became our new 'families' and we mastered new ways of socialising, learning and collaborating across a two metre void. For the pupils who didn't return, home-schooling continued.

It has been a steep learning curve for us all.

Nicky's story

I watched the pandemic unfold across the media before South Africa took decisive, early action. A State of Disaster was declared ten days after our first confirmed case was reported, and we went into a hard lockdown eleven days later when the country had over four hundred cases. The police and military were deployed. Alcohol and tobacco were banned. Exercise outside one's own property was forbidden. The #StayAtHome order stood for everything but essentials: food, pharmaceuticals and emergency visits to the doctor's and vet's.

Aside from flattening the curve to give the country time to prepare its medical services, the imposed bans served to lessen the usual alcohol-fuelled caseload that hits our emergency wards at weekends and prevent the sharing of the virus via bottles and cigarettes. Unlike Europe, the UK or the US, the spread of SARS-CoV-2 into South Africa's many densely populated and impoverished townships (where many people suffer from TB, HIV, diabetes and hypertension) pointed to a runaway wildfire of a sort that would make the New York death toll seem moderate.

The decisive action taken by Cyril Ramaphosa was bold and brave. Even his usual detractors saluted him as, for the first time in years, we saw real leadership and statesmanship. In the face of coronavirus the nation stood united – an unusual situation for South Africans to find themselves in, other than during international sporting events.

While many bought into the lockdown, others showed us how very difficult it is to effect when up to ten family members share a tiny shack built right up against their neighbour's home, where communal ablutions are common and there's no such thing as personal space, and where sharing is a means of survival. In the leafy suburbs with gated security estates and three to five bedroom homes set in treed gardens, we saw an altogether different approach: the complete refusal to comply, and entirely on the basis of perceived privilege and entitlement. Those residents carried on regardless, not because they couldn't adhere to lockdown, but because they wouldn't.

Discontent grew as the hard lockdown was extended from three weeks to five. It grew further as the risk-adjusted strategy moved us from Alert Level 5 to Alert Level 4. It grew on the back of obvious reasons – impacts on personal freedoms and resumption of economic activity – and also on the back of what one can only hope were unforeseen developments: bizarre commerce and trade regulations, police brutality and, critically, system failures and ongoing corruption that risked people dying not of Covid-19 but of starvation. The stark reality of the pandemic in South Africa is that it is impossible to separate it from the quagmire of politics and the legacy of nearly ten years of corruption that has all but destroyed the economy and State systems.

The first thing that became obvious to those of us in the Non-Profit sector was that lockdown meant economic hardship for the most vulnerable in South Africa's many impoverished communities. And by hardship, I mean starvation. Normal sources of income, much of it piecemeal, dried up overnight. Many hadn't applied for or didn't qualify for social grants. And it transpired that South Africa's welfare system was not only woefully inadequate but in greater disarray than the President appeared to have realised, with corruption still running rife. Eight weeks into lockdown, government food aid was not reaching those in most desperate need, and at eleven weeks there is still no sign of it. Anger has waxed and waned, as has the inevitable racial tension, particularly in light of the #blacklivesmatter movement. The Opposition has tried to make much mileage out of this – by taking a right-wing spin that plays to white fears – but aside from opposition politics, internal politics are also at play. There are still elements of the old regime in Cyril Ramaphosa's cabinet, and he fights not only the virus but political machinations within his own party.

On the flipside of political shenanigans, and in rapid response to desperate need, we saw a remarkable food-aid drive led by ordinary citizens and any number of Non-Profits. People came together to support those who had nothing. Admittedly, there were indications that for the privileged this was their feel-good moment of ego-driven conscience. Restaurant chefs and craft breweries created vast quantities of soup, and public school mums got their hands dirty and made mounds of sandwiches. (Some even included pricey, shop-bought ready meals and Lindt chocolates for a populace that usually survives on maize meal.) If nothing else, this particular generosity showed the very real divide and disconnect between South Africa's haves and have-nots.

While friends Marie-Kondo'd their homes and binge-watched Netflix, my own lockdown has focused on disseminating relevant information into local communities and finding ways to fundraise for food relief. I have worked up to thirteen hours a day, seven days a week. It has been exhausting and frustrating, and dealing with the growing complaints of the entitled, when juxtaposed with the tens of thousands starving, is simply nauseating.

The coronavirus pandemic has revealed the deep divisions in all our societies. In South Africa we have seen a clear divide between those willing to adhere to lockdown regulations and those who want lockdown ended, often on the back of not just economics but any number of conspiracy theories and opposition politics. The former see no return to normal, the latter are intent on normal's return. I believe any return to normal will be to our own cost, and the ongoing cost of our planet. If there is one thing that this pandemic asks us to heed, it is that we learn to live more kindly and gently upon the Earth. The way in which our economic systems are structured needs to change. The vast divide between very rich and very poor needs to shrink. The way in which we engage with each other needs to alter. Discrimination needs to end. We need to address the way we live in the world and with each other. And yet it is already apparent that those who have the most to lose will fight back in hard and ugly ways.

I'm mindful that most of the behaviour we see is fear-driven, irrespective of which side it comes from. There are those who fear for their health and their lives and that of their loved ones. There are those who fear the loss of their economic livelihoods, the restriction of their civil liberties and the rise of both a global and a local draconian authoritarianism. With the Opposition calling for more lockdown regulations to be lifted, while encouraging supporters to break the law, and with South Africa's move to Alert Level 3 on 1st June, we are galloping, as I write, towards our first peak. Despite every effort to contain SARS-CoV-2, it seems that my hometown may yet be on its way to a New York scenario.

Nick's story

We were leading a very full life. Our older two children were at university, our younger two approaching GCSEs. My wife was travelling all over the UK, delivering author visits in schools, and I was teaching music at conservatoire level, with a flourishing freelance practice in London.

And then Covid-19 began to loom.

My wife was a fortnight ahead of a government too bogged-down with Brexit to see the storm clouds. We began to isolate.

Almost at once there was a feeling of all-pervading calm. The busyness of our life ceased, and we settled into a strange tranquillity. Suddenly we had time to breathe, time to enjoy our children and each other, time to talk to friends and relatives, time to work out what was important to us and what we wanted in the future.

My work continued online. The close contact I had enjoyed with my students was gone, but there was so much more breathing space.

Several weeks in, life is slower and gentler than it was before. We live in the country with space around us. If we were living in a tenement flat in an inner city, I suspect our oasis would feel more like a prison.

But all oases have their boundaries, and after a period of great contentment, we are starting to become aware of what we miss: the beauty of the Lake District; trips to concerts and the theatre; our holidays in Spain and Suffolk.

We shall all, at some point, need to escape. But can we? The government might wish it to be so, but what rational discussion can one have with an unpredictable virus? We are pitted against an unthinking, undiscriminating chain of cells which has rendered mankind impotent.

Is this Nature's revenge for how we have treated our planet, exploiting its natural resources, destroying its forests, and depleting and poisoning its oceans?

At the very least, this is a stark warning – if not, indeed, a judgement.

Peter's story

I can remember quite clearly my last days of feeling well. I was going to say feeling 'normal' – but there was nothing normal about that time in March just before the country began its quarantine. There was the sense that something inevitable was about to occur, akin perhaps to what a civilian population feels before a war breaks out: a sense of helplessness, fear and a desire to get it over with, as we heard of country after country across Europe closing their borders and ordering their people indoors. Would we be next? How long until the government bowed to the inevitable? Why weren't we locked down already?

A huge debate opened up about what we should do for the best. Were the strains of 'Happy Birthday', hummed at sinks across the land, really going to be enough to prevent a disease little of us knew anything about and even fewer understood? News reports were suddenly full of strange terms and phrases like R numbers, social distancing and herd immunity.

Ah, herd immunity! The notion that the young and fit should be allowed to become infected in order to protect the more vulnerable. A policy that was proposed as a way of keeping the economy moving whilst some 'took it on the chin'.

Well, I was one of that herd. I acquired the virus in those couple of weeks before the UK was locked down. I was young(ish) and fit, and had no underlying health issues, so my chin was unwittingly offered as a sacrifice before epidemiological modelling showed that perhaps it might not be the best move to allow 400,000 people to die.

My last day of wellness was a Tuesday: for me this was Day 0. I'd been working away for a couple of weeks and was glad to be coming home. With the inevitable inertia that was hanging over us all, now was the time to be with my wife and children. The train was eerily quiet, especially compared to the standing-room-only journey I'd taken the week before. Then, social distancing had not entered the everyday lexicon: the guy in front of me was coughing and spluttering, and the guy behind was sniffing.

My relief to be home quickly gave way to exhaustion. I opted for an early night. Apparently I was quite restless when my wife came to bed, so she slept in the spare room. Thank goodness she did.

The following morning I woke up unrefreshed and went back to sleep. The hours and days began to merge, and my journey with Covid-19 began, a companion which has treated me to an advent-calendar-like revelation of novel surprises for the last 67 days.

Its first gift was a fever. I began to get very hot and then very cold. I also started feeling weird. It was flu-like in its prickliness but unlike any flu I'd had before. Every nerve in my body felt like it was fizzing, and something deep-down seemed out-of-kilter. I had stomach cramps and nausea plus some dizziness. I guessed I was ill, but as I had no cough or sore throat and the symptoms were mainly gastrointestinal I assumed it was food poisoning or possibly a stomach bug. Nonetheless, I chose to remain in my room and use our en suite bathroom to shield the family.

In the early hours of what I think was Saturday morning, I felt the sudden urge to vomit and made my way to the toilet. I remember leaning forwards and lifting the lid, but my next recollection was coming round on the floor on the other side of the room, my knee and elbow oozing blood. Clearly, I'd passed out. I crawled back to bed and lay there shaking uncontrollably. Somebody hung a packet of bagels on the back of the bedroom door and once I could move I tried to eat.

For the next seventy-two hours I remained in bed. I became aware that I couldn't see out of my left eye. I had developed extreme conjunctivitis, something which was not yet on the publicised list of Covid symptoms.

By Day 6 I felt well enough to try and get up. Around teatime I ventured downstairs for the first time in almost a week. The looks I was given by my son and my wife told me all I needed to know. Pale, thin and sporting a matted, shut left eye is hardly an ideal picture of health.

Over the next three days I dared to hope I was getting better. Obviously I'd had a bug, but as none of the symptoms had been flagged as those of Covid and I hadn't had a 'new continuous cough', I believed it must just have been a gastric infection.

With hindsight, I can see that my being away for over a week before starting with symptoms and isolating myself in the bedroom for six days almost certainly spared my wife and teenagers. But this was by accident rather than design. Fortunately, the country was by now in lockdown so the need for family isolation was made easier and became somewhat self-fulfilling.

My evening meal on Day 8 was rounded off with a sudden pain in my chest. My daughter, who was sitting opposite me, looked a little alarmed, but I reassured her (and myself) that it was just indigestion. As I stood up I was noticeably dizzy and by the time I got to the sofa the 'weird' feeling had returned. I went back to bed.

During Days 9, 10 and 11 my fever came back, and my chest pain got worse. I contacted 111. It was suggested that I might have Covid but as I had no difficulty breathing and my fever had by now abated, I was advised not to go to the doctor or the hospital. Nor was there any chance of getting tested.

By Day 17 I had begun to feel better again. The chest pain had eased, and my gastrointestinal issues had resolved, though I did have a very peculiar brain fog. I couldn't focus on anything for long and couldn't remember details from the preceding days.

I contacted my brother-in-law to compare notes. He'd started with symptoms about a week before me, and his experience was worse than mine. He'd had serious breathing difficulties and had almost called an ambulance on a couple of occasions. He was now on the mend and put his more severe case down to having taken ibuprofen before it was suggested this might not be a good idea. We sympathised with each other's plights and marvelled at our wonderful and remarkably resilient wives, and he reassured me that as I was now feeling better I was surely through the worst.

But by the early evening of Day 18, I was feeling weird again. This time I had a burning sensation in my stomach, lower abdomen and urethra. I went back to bed but couldn't sleep. Over the next few hours the pain got worse and my fever returned.

I called my GP in the morning, who confirmed that I almost certainly had Covid and possibly a secondary infection, most likely viral. I was told to take paracetamol and keep regular track of my temperature. She said she would ring me the next morning and advised me to call 999 if I got worse or developed breathing difficulties. She actually called again that evening, which was both reassuring and disconcerting.

The next day another GP from the surgery rang to check on my progress. She suggested I try some antibiotics.

Day 23 was Easter Sunday, usually one of my favourite days of the year. I was able to get out of bed and even managed some online socialising. I appeared to be recovering.

For the next ten days I made slow but steady progress…but the advent calendar doors were not yet exhausted. On Day 32 I noticed an uncomfortable area in my lower left ribcage. Over the following four days, the pain in my abdomen eased and the pain in my ribcage grew with an almost seesaw-like symmetry. Like a pernicious weed the pain intensified and spread its tendrils across the whole of my ribcage and back.

I rang the GP again. This time the conclusion was that I might have strained a rib or intercostal muscle and that it would probably settle down. As I wasn't having any breathing difficulties, I should take more paracetamol and call back the following week. I did explain that I still felt a bit ill, but that was ascribed to post viral fatigue. If I'd had Covid, I should be over it by now.

By Day 38 everything I ate tasted of metal. This was now being reported as a possible symptom, so was the virus still present in my body after all?

My question was answered the following day. As I reached for my phone to pick up a text message, I was suddenly aware that I couldn't breathe properly. I lay on my back and tried to take a deep breath. I was panting now and even my deepest breaths couldn't provide my lungs with enough air.

That's when I began to get scared.

Imagine the feeling you get when you have a blocked nose with a bad cold and just can't seem to get a large-enough breath. Well, transfer that to your lungs. That's the closest comparison I can muster.

I lay there struggling to breathe and began to panic. I shook involuntarily, and as the panic gripped my muscles I could sense my breathing becoming even more laboured. My mind was whirling. Was it the breathlessness causing the panic or vice versa?

I reached for my phone and called my wife, and as I did so I sat up on the side of the bed. Immediately my breathing began to feel slightly easier. We discussed calling an ambulance but as the panic began to subside I felt in charge of my breathing again, even though I was still finding it hard to get the air in. I decided to go to the bathroom before planning my next move. As I stood up, my breathing cleared. Free from the pressure of lying down, my lungs felt full again. Perhaps I wouldn't need an ambulance after all.

I still felt very shaky, so putting the whole incident down to a panic attack, I lay down on my side to give my body a chance to recover. I fell asleep immediately.

About an hour later I awoke, relieved to be alive. The ribcage pain was bad, and it was clearly affecting a much wider area than before, but at least when I stood up I could breathe.

Yet again, I called the GP. This time the doctor suggested I probably had either costochondritis or pleurisy. I was prescribed paracetamol and rest.

A doctor friend suggested I get hold of a fingertip blood oxygen meter. These small devices cost around £25 online and measure the amount of oxygen in the blood via a non-invasive UV light. They have proved excellent early-warning tools (along with thermometers and blood pressure monitors) for patients with Covid. They gauge whether a patient might be suffering from hypoxia (a lack of oxygen in the blood) which has been one of the major complications of the disease. Mine arrived on Day 41 and I began a twice-daily routine of checking my blood pressure, blood oxygen and body temperature.

And, boy, was it needed! The feeling of being unable to breathe was without doubt the scariest sensation I have ever experienced. Always in the back of my mind was the knowledge that oxygen is essential to life. Every time I lay down over the following three weeks, my lungs felt the return of that hopeless blocked-nose sensation. It was only the reassurance of the oximeter that stopped me from calling 999 on several occasions.

One night was especially difficult. The pleuritic pain was excruciating, and as I struggled to get comfortable, my breathing began to get even trickier. My oxygen levels were OK, but the sensation was very disconcerting. Every muscle of my body ached for sleep, and my eyes were heavy, but as I closed them, I touched my wife next to me, and for the only time in my life genuinely wondered if I would ever wake up again.

As the days of living with this illness have turned into weeks, much has changed. I am writing this on Day 67 and am not yet back to full health. My breathing is better but still laboured at night when lying down. Even sitting to watch television is only managed with regular breaks to stand and fill my lungs again. The pain is with me constantly, both in my ribs and my joints. It is less extreme, but a chronic reminder that I'm still playing host to this new and very unwelcome guest.

A couple of weeks ago I was referred to some social media groups set up by sufferers with similar tales of longer-term symptoms. It was a relief to find that I wasn't alone, and that my pattern of symptoms wasn't unusual. So-called 'long-tail' cases are only now being properly recognised by the medical profession and many of us are being invited to become involved in studies. Whether our ongoing symptoms are caused by the virus or our own immune systems is as yet unknown. Similar levels of ignorance surround the long-term effects we may go on to experience.

The very nature of a novel virus means that we are making fresh discoveries every day. When I began my odyssey, the only commonly-known symptoms were a dry, continuous cough, a fever and possibly breathing difficulties. Now, of course, the list stretches across several pages, from nausea and gastrointestinal symptoms to conjunctivitis, muscle and joint pain, fatigue, brain fog, panic attacks, delirium, memory loss, skin rashes and an altered or lost sense of smell and taste, plus a cornucopia of others. People who catch it now will at least know better what to expect and hopefully wider testing will help stop them spreading it further.

I owe so much to the love, care and understanding of my family, especially my wonderful wife. Also to the careful help and guidance of the NHS and the support of friends and colleagues. Like the virus, I am a novelty to many, and everyone wants to know what it's really like.

How long my unwanted companion will be squatting in my body is still unknown, but after several false dawns I no longer tell people that I'm getting better. So as not to jinx any genuine progress, I tell them instead, "I'm getting there."

It would be a cliché to refer to an experience like mine as life-changing, but it has certainly been an education. In the twenty-first century, many of us in the West take our health for granted. We put our faith in the hands of our health-care systems, believing that most problems can be fixed. But we don't have to look very far back to see that it hasn't always been so. My own grandfather died of pneumonia in the late 1930s, before antibiotics were widely available, something that led my mother to have a lifelong fear of getting wet and cold. I never really understood her anxiety before but having had an illness that has no known cure, I now appreciate where her fear came from.

I feel like I've been an unwitting – yet very generous and patient – landlord. Let's hope that when my tenant eventually departs, the mess it leaves behind is not too ugly and that any damage is cleared up, leaving me good as new.

Anupma's story

13th January

Saw patients in my London GP surgery today who were worried about contracting Covid after their families abroad had been in the plague.

One, who was wearing a mask and gloves, was staring down at the Cantonese dialogue on her phone. Her eyes held an expression I would come to see again and again, either in person or on video: anxious, bereaved, fearful and alone.

Still waiting to hear back from Public Health on Covid guidance.

7th February

Dr Li Wenliang died, and my Doctor's Facebook group mourned.

Local leadership is really struggling to tessellate as communications are centralised, in spite of our protestations. We have transferred all our services online and reluctantly handed over the care of our patients to NHS 111.

9th March

Read the horrific tweets by Dr Daniele Macchini, the Italian ITU doctor.

First suspected Covid death in the practice.

***

By this time, we individual clinicians had trawled though scientific information, briefings and data in order to make decisions about how to look after our patients, colleagues, families and communities. We were aware that the government was being too slow, and no guidance was forthcoming.

Over the next two weeks, our workforce was reduced to a tenth because of fever and the need to isolate. I was travelling to other surgeries to cover, which was terrifying as the infection control procedures still hadn't been standardised.

My friend's father died. Then another friend's lover. Many of us refer to this period as "those awful two weeks".

We knew we were going to lose some patients, and I remember worrying about one lovely lady in particular. Out in reception, I shed a silent tear for her. I think that was the moment the staff realised what was coming – and that perhaps I was human after all.

We worked with teams to ensure that all our sick and vulnerable patients were contacted. GPs have done care plans and discussed End of Life Scenarios for years, but now there was a suggestion we would have to ration care. The ethical dilemmas were a minefield.

We continued to accelerate our understanding of the disease, and protocols were created which spread like wildfire. We were on call every hour of the day either working or researching – together, but also very much on our own.

And then I got Covid…

***

Thursday 26th March

I was lying in bed, exhausted and lonely, contemplating whether I'd be able to get fruit and vegetables for the kids and thinking about the patients I had admitted that day.

I heard a clattering outside and dragged myself towards the noise. My children explained that people were clapping for the NHS and I became very emotional. My WhatsApp was beeping like mad with colleagues telling me what was going on. That night many NHS workers were humbled by the cushion of support that the public placed firmly beneath us in our hour of need.

I thought of the bus drivers, the key workers, the police, the chemists, the coroners...

***

NHS England was struggling to reverse the deep fragmentation caused by ten years of austerity, and The Long Term Plan was attempting to address inequalities. It is no surprise to any doctor that wealth inequality is the biggest predictor of disease, and Covid deaths really stamped themselves on our deprived area of London.

Patients who made it home frequently required a lot of domiciliary monitoring. The waiting room (usually packed) was now restricted to a maximum of five people wearing masks, and Monica's room with its beautiful floor-length window was reserved for the donning and doffing of PPE.

Then the phone calls started coming in:

"I don't know if I should bother you with this..." (another possible cancer).

"I have back pain and my period hasn't come." (Ectopic pregnancies still kill women.)

"If my neighbour hadn't seen me, I would have leapt off the balcony." (Suicide prevention has always been a significant part of a GP's job, and during Covid more patients than usual took their own lives, despite our proactive phone calls.)

The work rolled in. Staff casualties rolled in. Grief whirled around the surgery.

***

15th May

Had a wobble at work, trying to deal with three complicated young psychiatric emergencies. Feel unheard by central government.

Contacted study group.

18th June

Like childbirth or a bad flight, I seem to have compartmentalised the traumas of the last three months, although the loss of some of my colleagues has burnt a permanent hole in my heart.

GPs are used to fighting on behalf of their patients and we really did protect them in all this, rather than simply adhere to mindless generic protocols. Now we have our patients back: the families; the children; the survivors; the bereaved; the unrepatriated. We will recover, forward-plan, get out the retrospectroscope, publish, communicate and improve.

I would like to keep my PPE close by me for the rest of my career. I shall continue to protect my patients, colleagues, family and friends, and the general public. I want to say thank you to every single one of them...because these are the people who protected me.

Lily's story

Washington DC, March 2020

Has your chewing always been this loud? It's truly unbearable. Oh well, at least it's time to go to work. Up the stairs. In a little corner. There are signs on the door: WORKING – TRY AGAIN LATER! And: ON A CALL! Another is simpler: GO AWAY! Sometimes they are regarded.

All of the children are home. All of everyone's children are home. It's the greatest homecoming in memory, like returning for Christmas – only possibly to stay forever. Mine are none of them children, of course, and thank God for that. Our youngest is 14 and finished school online, so we are now moving into 'Summer Break'. Break? Summer?

I remember we used to 'travel' before all this – to see others and enjoy their company. Now we speak of where we will be able to go and be distant from them. We're all turning into transcendentalist poets, looking for our Walden Pond to be alone on, together. With the same people we've spent the last five hundred years with. All I want is other people. When the weather is pleasant, we meet in 'driveway parties': potluck, with chairs pulled far apart. These moments are a treasure.

The house is unspeakably grimy: when I talk to my friends, we agree that all our houses are unspeakably grimy. We absolutely cannot care about it. I have conference calls with colleagues, delighting in the way nobody cares anymore if all five dogs are barking or a naked toddler blazes through the room while we sort out the proper disposition of intellectual property assets in a bankruptcy. "Have they sent over the schedule of patent registrations? MOMMY, I ATE A CRICKET! Bark bark bark bark bark! Tell Daddy, darling. So, about those licenses…" On social media, it's completely bananas: we swing from hilarious banality to The End Times a thousand times a day. I dip in periodically, then tune out for ages. It's just too much.

What will we do for lunch? No idea what you're doing, because if I have to be near you chewing one more time, I won't be responsible for my actions. Also, your beard makes me want to call you "Pa-paw", like we're from the mountains. Are you out to shoot some squirrel?

At the same time, there is a pleasure in there being literally nothing going on for weeks and weeks and weeks. There are no engagements to dodge, no cocktail networking receptions, not even church. Nothing but work and family and distanced friends and games and Netflix and too much ice cream and sleep and more work. I love not commuting. I see the changes already: we won't go back to doing it every day, because we know we can work remotely. I pray that all this insanity will lead us to a saner life, somehow.

But in the meantime: GO AWAY!

Emily's story

I have never been overly concerned about my health. I eat fairly well and do enough exercise. But at the start of lockdown I became a hypochondriac. Whenever I had the smallest ache or pain, I truly believed it was something life-threatening.

The feelings I was experiencing – a sore jaw and neck, stomach pains and a tight chest – were actually due to anxiety. The jaw and neck problem, for example, was caused by me unconsciously clenching my muscles throughout the day and in my sleep.

I was overwhelmed by thoughts of death, and regularly imagined myself – or people close to me – becoming severely ill. I felt as though I was losing control of my own mind as my thoughts raced from one horror to the next. I have never experienced anxiety like it, and was constantly monitoring the way I felt, hypersensitive to anything that didn't feel right and obsessively googling my symptoms. I slept badly and developed some fairly unhealthy behaviours as a result of the stress and anxiety. This has improved a little now, but there are still days when the feelings come flooding back.

Another stress has come from my studies. I'm in my second year at university and have had four major assignments due in during lockdown. I have found it extremely difficult to concentrate and find the motivation to start work. It's ironic, since one of the things I have had lectures on recently is exactly that: motivation for learning – and, specifically, what prevents it. In essence, I am learning about why I cannot finish simple tasks, and why my work cannot possibly be my best.

One of the things I have studied is Maslow's Hierarchy of Needs. This is a pyramid-shaped model made up of various sections, at the top of which is 'self-actualisation', the ability to solve problems and be creative (two things essential to me completing my university assignments). An individual cannot reach self-actualisation until they have secured the sections lower down the pyramid, including the 'physiological' and 'safety' sections, which include things like sleep, good health (and that of one's family members) and security of employment. No wonder I can't be successful at a time like this!

It's especially hard experiencing these difficult emotions without the one person I would usually share them with. I am isolating at my family home with my parents, so I'm apart from my boyfriend of two-and-a-half years. Talking to someone else just isn't the same. Video-calling doesn't cut it: the blurred lagging images; the 'poor connection' screen; the waiting for replies.

That said, there have been a few positives to come out of lockdown. I've spent more time with my mum than ever before: we have breakfast together and take it in turns to cook. Sometimes we sit in the same room and do different things without speaking to one another. Just having someone there is really comforting. I feel sorry for people who live by themselves: it must be so lonely.

I have also discovered a new appreciation for nature and poetry. I enjoy reading poetry in the arbour at the end of the garden, especially when the sun is out. I also try to go for a walk by the river near my house two or three times a week, where there are many beautiful flowers and few people…the best ratio.

Anna's story

We finally shut the doors to the public on 23rd March. No vicar ever wants to have to do that, and we certainly didn't want to at Salisbury Cathedral at the start of lockdown. An open door, especially in an ancient building like this one, is symbolic. It gives you a foretaste, preparing you for the story that's about to unfold inside. With its iconic spire, the Cathedral is a wonderful and lively place, welcoming visitors from all over the world as well as regular worshippers. Although we were expecting it by then, it was still a huge shock to watch the Head Verger lock up that evening, as we politely said goodbye and asked the final visitors to leave.

Normally, there isn't a single day of the year when the Cathedral is closed. Its statutes state that services should be said or sung every morning and evening, as a minimum. I started working there just over a year ago. Getting used to a busy and demanding new job, I often found myself rushing over from my office to the daily service of Evensong with only five minutes to spare. This regular walk through the Cloister and into the hushed Cathedral soon became one of the most magical parts of my day, one of the things I love most about my job – and I miss it a lot.

As the Cathedral Precentor (Latin for 'first singer', the priest who leads the choir in the sung responses), I'm responsible for the liturgy and music. That includes the content and choreography of church services and involves working closely with the Cathedral musicians. It's been an enormous challenge to put all our services online, but there have been some gains too. Almost overnight we had to start videoing ourselves leading and giving our sermons, with the Cathedral choir recording the musical parts of the services on their own at home, to be stitched together later. Some of our attempts at live streaming have been hilarious, like trying to give a serious spiritual daily reflection whilst sideways on to the viewer.

Before lockdown, my team and I had been working hard on a big service to celebrate the 800th anniversary of the laying of the foundation stones of the Cathedral on 28th April. The full capacity of Salisbury Cathedral is 1,800 and it felt very strange not to be able to celebrate this significant moment in the building itself. We quickly had to form a different plan, but our digital service attracted thousands of worshippers virtually from around the world. Putting our worship online has allowed us to be more inventive in some ways. Looking back, I can't believe how far we've come in such a short space of time.

Before the anniversary service came Holy Week and Easter, the most important week in the Christian year. It was sad, in my first year, not to be able to celebrate this in the normal way, but it was even harder for the choristers. Aged between 7 and 13, they are expected to perform daily as professionals alongside the adult singers of the choir. Singing together is part of their identity. To have this suddenly taken away was tough, especially for those preparing to leave this summer and go to new schools. But they have brought comfort through their singing to even more people than before.

Online worship has helped us reach people during a difficult time. Working in a busy cathedral is very different from working in a parish church. With a larger congregation, it can take longer to get to know people well. But this is one of the most rewarding aspects of ministry, and during the lockdown, as a clergy team, we've prioritised pastoral care, staying in close touch with parishioners, especially those who are vulnerable, phoning and emailing them often. People have reacted in different ways, and I've got to know them on a deeper level. At the first Zoom daily prayer service, it was moving to see familiar faces, including a man who can't normally come to the Cathedral now participating from his bed. It's taken lockdown to make us realise how easy it is, really, to provide church services that can be accessed by everyone, anywhere.

Lockdown has raised many questions, such as whether celebrating communion or making wedding vows online are valid. But Christianity and other religions have always adapted to new technologies. Digital services are not new. The first online church service was held before the World Wide Web was even invented, after the Challenger space shuttle tragically exploded just after take-off in 1986 and a small Presbyterian community set up a memorial event online. I've certainly learned a lot over these last few months. Meeting together online will never be a substitute for seeing one another in the flesh, but online services are set to continue. Even when we can hold services in the Cathedral again, our worship will look very different.

Tomorrow, 15th June, a small area of the Cathedral will re-open for individuals to come into and pray or reflect and light a candle. It's nothing like the level of activity we had before, but I'm still excited. It's taken a lot of preparation and careful planning to get to this point, and I can't wait to see people again. Of all the different activities that normally coexist, including sightseeing and grand services, simply offering a space for prayer brings us back to our core purpose.

The Cathedral has been through tough times before. The Archbishop of Canterbury, Justin Welby, had been due to attend our big 800th anniversary celebration, and it was comforting to discover that, on the original foundation day in April 1220, the then-Archbishop never made it either, having been detained negotiating with the Welsh at Shrewsbury. But the celebration still went ahead anyway. It's incredible to think that the Cathedral has been there ever since, adapting to new situations: a sign of hope on the horizon.

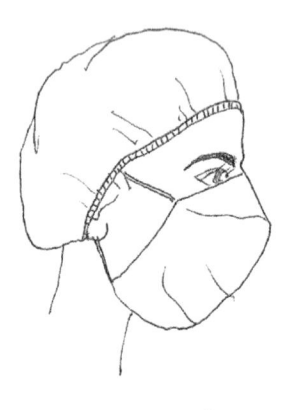

Josh's story

I'm a Year 10 student, and things have changed a lot for me under lockdown. I no longer have to wake up at 6.30 to get the bus to school, but I miss my mates and I really miss being able to go out at the weekends.

I also miss real lessons. I have to create my own structure, and online learning takes a bit of getting used to. I usually get up and have a wash by 10, and then do an hour's work before lunch, followed by two hours in the afternoon. My Maths lessons take the form of answering questions online, whereas others (Geography, for example) are done using PowerPoints. Most of my teachers have been very good about setting work and I'm not worried about falling behind because we're all in this together. Basically, though, I'm having to learn to be my own teacher – and that's hard.

I'm definitely getting to spend a lot more time with my family. My sister is back from university and it's been nice hanging out with her. My parents drag me out to do chores in the garden, and I play quite a bit of table tennis with my brother. There's the odd fight about ownership of the Xbox, but mostly we get on fine. I'm definitely doing more cooking than normal!

When this is all over, I'm looking forward to going on holiday, seeing my mates and returning to my Saturday job.

Katrina's story

He bit me. He bit me hard. The nurse standing next to me said my scream stayed with her for ages. But no pain registered. Only the fear of him never letting go, the fear of him biting right through my flesh.

I'm a mental health worker at a psychiatric intensive care unit, a high security ward for those who have become a danger to themselves or society. It's an intense environment, and I am constantly on my guard, ready to diffuse explosive situations – but it's a job I love.

Lockdown has made many of us fearful. Our liberty has been taken away overnight, stripping us of everyday choices and snatching us up in a gigantic wave of anxiety and paranoia. As a mental health worker, life hasn't stopped. Shifts continue and the intensity of the work increases as we struggle with the physical challenges of wearing PPE for twelve solid hours a day.

For our patients, every day is lockdown. Some are exhausted by the voices chattering away inside their heads. Some are paranoid, terrified of leaving their delusional worlds to inhabit the real one. Some beg us to let them kill themselves. These people have little or no liberty, and very few choices. Trust doesn't come easily to them, because throughout their lives they have been let down too often by the people who should have kept them safe. They rely heavily on family visits, which have currently been suspended. And the friendly, smiling staff they have come to depend upon have morphed into masked beings. I was relieved when one patient told me that he could still tell when I was smiling. "Your eyes are brighter, and your wrinkles are more noticeable," he said.

On a personal level, the lockdown has had its positives. Our five children are now all teenagers or in their early twenties, and time spent with them is so precious. Their empathy for the patient who bit me was extraordinary: they showed real understanding of how someone's mental health can be destroyed to the point where they lose control.

The patients are not without insight, either. A few weeks ago, it was ice-cream for pudding at the unit. One man suddenly leapt to his feet and ran to the counter, asking for water. "Have you eaten it too quickly?" I asked, laughing. "Have you got brain freeze?" He drank two cups, then turned and looked me straight in the eye. "Yes," he replied. "That's why I'm here."

Ben's story

It started so suddenly. The previous week I had met a group of friends in the Agordo Piazza and suggested we had our apperitivi outside and observed the recommended social distancing rules. They laughed at me. A week later we were all locked down and paranoid.

We had already debated leaving our home in Italy for our house in Greece, but the advice from friends who lived there was not to come. The majority of the locals are over 70 and have underlying health problems, so the idea of a family arriving from northern Italy sent panic through the village. We decided to stay in our little stone house in the Dolomites.

We were lucky in so many respects: we had each other, and our mischievous four-year-old, Max, kept us entertained. Our holiday business, 'Pretty Greek Villas', had experienced a really good run leading up to the lockdown, so there was no need to worry. It would, I said, be 'a forced sabbatical'. Hopefully we'd make it back to Greece in a few months and spend the summer relaxing by the pool…

I read an article by a war correspondent who had spent a lot of time in isolation. Her advice was to allow oneself a period of time to adapt, and not to make endless lists of exercise plans or tasks to achieve. So I enjoyed taking Max for walks in the forest and down by the river. As the colours of spring swept through the valley, we practised our aim throwing stones at a stump that stuck out from one of the eddies, surrounded by snowy Dolomite peaks. The moments we shared were lovely and a great antidote to the daily news of rising case numbers and deaths.

Italy was at the epicentre of the pandemic for months. Clear rules were put in place and things were taken very seriously, right down to the little bags containing masks that were tied to people's doors.

We decided that I should be the one to go out for provisions. At first it was very intimidating. No more than fifteen shoppers were allowed into the supermarket at any one time, and everyone had to wear masks and gloves. The tobacconist accepted only one person, as did the wine shop. Bottles of hand gel and disinfectant sprays were located at each commercial entrance and everyone followed the rules.

My wife was kept busy dealing with clients who hadn't taken out the necessary holiday insurance, and we also had to deal with anxious villa owners who rely on the income from the rentals we sell. Talk about piggy-in-the-middle!

The messages coming from BBC World News were unclear. Airlines wouldn't function normally for three years, but perhaps some kind of safe tunnel connection might be established. The WHO cried, "Test, test, test!" But what exactly did that mean? Test who? For what? Which test? Where are the tests?

I started to worry about how long we could sustain ourselves and spent several sleepless nights turning it all over in my mind. *The holiday business is finished! What the hell can I do instead? Do I have the energy and commitment to make a new start? What a nightmare! So much for a sabbatical! So much for making it back to Greece! The phone never stops, the emails never stop, we're working harder than normal and not making a penny and somehow it's all our fault the clients didn't buy insurance...* With the click of a button I shut off our monthly advertising cost and calculated we could keep going for about eighteen months.

What is this Covid-19? Is it really the killer the scientists predicted? Or is it just something for the middle classes to get paranoid about? What about the countries that can't afford to furlough their inhabitants? We might not know much about coronavirus, but we do know what happens when people starve. We know what cholera looks like. Typhoid. Domestic violence. Civil unrest.

I liked my life before the bug escaped from a bat cave somewhere in China. I care about the poor and I try to run my life on principle, but I like my long ski seasons and travelling around Greece in search of new opportunity. I like being productive and creative. I don't mind wearing a mask and taking precautions, and I don't mind keeping my distance – but please, lockdown makes no sense anymore! You can't detach public health from the economy, and my poor little boy hasn't seen his friends for months and has developed a twitch.

Three weeks out of lockdown, Brits still can't come to our villas in Greece, but the Greeks can! And the Swiss and the Israelis and soon the Italians, too. We've spent a little money on advertising, and some bookings have been made – but we can't get back home ourselves. We're through the worst, though.

Or are we? We don't really know, do we? Nobody knows anything. Giuseppe Conte declared that Italy should continue in lockdown until a vaccine is found, but it can't afford to do that. In Greece, Kyriakos Mitsotakis was praised for his good management of locking down early, but the country badly needs tourism to start working again. As for the UK – well, the world is laughing at the appalling way the virus has been managed there. STAY ALERT, CONTROL THE VIRUS, SAVE LIVES. I'm still amazed they haven't changed that slogan. Two weeks of quarantine on your return from abroad, when Britain has been the worst affected! It doesn't make sense.

Mind you, none of this makes sense, and there's only one thing we can all say for certain. We weren't prepared.

Maybe next time…

Sophie's story

Lockdown feels like a hazy dream from which I haven't yet woken up. When it was announced, I was living at university with my housemates (the ones who hadn't already left). At first, I thought it would be an adventure, but after doing the same walk every day and struggling with my mental health, I soon realised I wanted to go home.

However, I didn't want to put my family – in particular, my elderly dad – at risk, so my parents found me a friend's caravan where I could quarantine before coming back. Although I didn't much like the idea of leaving my independent life at university to live in my childhood bedroom, I could see all the amazing things going home would bring: a break; time to rest; the company of my crazy-but-fun family; a big garden; a place to re-ground myself. The next day I found myself in the back of a taxi, feeling very uncertain about the future.

Once in the caravan, reality set in. For two weeks I would be little more than a hibernating animal. It was incredibly strange being in such a small space – and incredibly quiet, too. I grew accustomed to the sound of birdsong. Figuring out how to keep myself occupied was a challenge, to say the least, and the first few days were hard. Stephen Fry's *Harry Potter* audiobooks and the radio became my best friends. Every morning I would wake at 7 and go for my daily walk up the hill, where eight lunatic horses greeted me. When I got back, I would turn on the gas hob for my morning coffee and warm my hands. Each day would then follow roughly the same schedule: have a nap; listen to *Harry Potter;* have breakfast; listen to *Woman's Hour* (I am 20 – I can't believe I have reached that point); stare out of the window and contemplate life; read; think about lunch; make lunch; eat lunch; read some more; have a minor breakdown; have a cup of tea; listen to music and attempt to dance inside the caravan; read again; call people; have dinner; do yoga; tick off another day; go to bed.

I sometimes paced the caravan to get some more steps in, which made me dizzy. I expect the neighbours thought I'd lost it. I kept a journal, which highlights just how up-and-down the whole experience was. One entry reads: *'Not too long left now. Woke at 5:30 – it was freezing. Went for sunrise walk at 6.30. Very sunny and beautiful up on the hill. The trees are in full bloom now. Walked for an hour, listening to the last Harry Potter audiobook. Can't wait to get home.'* The final entry simply reads: *'I'VE DONE IT!'*

Being isolated definitely reminded me how lucky I am, and on the morning I went home, I felt like Rapunzel being let out of her tower. I sat outside in the garden with the sun on my face and the birds singing around me.

I know that quarantining myself was the right thing to do, but I wouldn't recommend it to anyone, and hope I'll never have to do anything like it again!

Tia's story

Home-schooling is the wish of loads of kids who hate their teachers. But it's not all it's cracked up to be, especially when you're still being taught by your normal teacher, everything's online and you can't go outside (much) because there's a global pandemic going on. At the time of writing it's Week I-Don't-Even-Know-What-Anymore of lockdown, and schools are closed. My school is using Purple Mash, a kids' online activity centre. It has a blog function, which the teachers use to tell us what work to do, plus a whole bunch of other activities that we would normally use once in a while for ICT or to stay occupied during Indoor Break.

I'm in Year 6, so I should be taking SATs this year. I wasn't worried about them because I tend to do well in school, but they're not the only thing that won't happen now. We were supposed to be putting on a play in the summer, and also had a residential trip to PGL that I was really looking forward to.

My life is especially weird at the moment because my mum is a key worker. She doesn't work for the NHS, and she's not risking her life in any way. She works for the Foreign Office and is helping with the emergency response (see *Samantha's story*). She does two night shifts a week, which means that for three days a week we only see her for half the day because she is asleep the rest of the time. In some ways this is better than usual because normally she leaves before we are up and comes back after 6pm, but it's hard that I can't talk to her even though she's in the house.

My little sister's birthday is in late April, so my parents came up with somewhere to 'go' – Longleat Safari Park had a virtual tour on their YouTube channel. I sorted out nearly everything else: I organised the 'party' (setting up a trail of safari-themed cuddly toys to make it more fun), decorated the living room (where the safari happened), made the cake (it took me two days!) and set up the birthday tea.

Talking of birthdays, a friend of mine also had one in lockdown. We went over to her house to deliver her present (a denim pocket-turned bag with her initial on the front) and had a great time. We played with her dog, saw her new scooter and chatted…all while outside and two metres apart. We nearly froze to death, but it was worth it.

I FaceTime and Skype my friends a lot, but nothing compares to real-life chatting. We have 'seen' loads of people I haven't set eyes on since I was tiny, including some friends from the US. The weekly 'Clap for Carers' has been fun too, and I hope that persists after the virus.

With everything that's going on, my life is very peculiar right now, but then I dare you to find someone whose isn't.

Minna's story

Part One

"How did it come to this?", the Leader of the Opposition asked the Prime Minister, when Britain reached the highest death rate in Europe. Every day, for ninety-five days, in total isolation, I have asked myself the same question.

How did it come to me wishing my parents a happy Golden Wedding Anniversary over the ether? How did it come to my only face-to-face contact being a medic giving me an injection at home to stop the searing agony in my body? How did it come to me being trapped in a first floor flat with nothing but orchids for company? How did it come to friendships being reduced to the click of a button on social media? It's not just the normal rhythm of life that has stopped. It's communication. It's everything that grounds our very existence.

Then I think of the green shoots that I saw growing on May morning, and the blossom. The birdsong, more urgent and insistent than ever; the bumble bees, that a year ago we thought would be lost forever, now happily making daily odysseys through wildflowers of every hue. Is that to be our new freedom: allowing what is normally curated and hidden away simply to grow?

If so, then I choose green space, catching my breath as Nature catches my soul, bruised but still here. I choose authentic connection with the people I love because I've been given a taste of what death is like. As a single, childless woman, I can see the world carrying on without me. Am I nothing but a memory now? Many times since March I have felt like a ghost with a pulse, but then a jolt comes: a message, a letter, a video call, a phone call – and I realise I can still feel my heart beating, my soul moving like a butterfly in a cage. No wonder the Greek word, psyche, means both soul and butterfly.

A friend introduces me to her toddler who now says "Mama" and "Hiya!". He looks me in the eye and beams at me through the screen, and I break down at the power of the connection. Because this is aliveness, despite the fact I don't know when I can hold this cherub-like boy in my arms. This is who we really are. This matters more than our status, our popularity, our routine. This is truth, this is love. *We* are truth. *We* are love. And I will never, ever take that for granted again.

Part Two

On my sunset walks to the peaceful green space where the trees and the birdsong form my haven, I watch as the sky turns to stars and the daisies close. I walk in places I would have been afraid to walk in before, and this notion reaches into every aspect of my life. I have been in the same environment and profession for twenty years, working myself into the ground, giving away the best years of my life – and at the expense of my joy. Always at the expense of my joy. Always that round peg in a square hole.

I knew, in this lockdown space that I was given – physically limited, yet in so many other ways limitless – that I could draw myself together and rethink everything. 'I am strong enough to start again' became my mantra.

What did you do during the 2020 lockdown? This will be the question for decades to come. Well, I found out how to make my soul sing again, how to live my best life. I gave up what no longer served me. I am about to enter a new profession – an extraordinary opportunity to pursue my true vocation of sharing what I love with the next generation of bright young women: to empower, to challenge and to nurture them. All that was lacking or lost in my last professional incarnation is, by contrast, gifted to me in abundance in my new one: a place of fresh starts, of belonging; a new city, new people, new reflections and refractions of the work I did before; introducing the joy to a far broader demographic.

That darkness I felt in early lockdown? It vanished, just as the night gave way to the dawn on my sunrise walks in June when I returned to the same spot I had spent sunset and saw the daisy open her petals to the light and the sun touch everything, illuminating the ordinary and transforming it into something to cherish: a spider's web; an oak leaf; a cloud; any and all possibilities.

Clare's story

On Monday 23rd March I left work in time to catch an early evening film. I knew things here in New Zealand were starting to change, and my response was to seek some escapism in Jane Austen's *Emma*. I had the whole cinema to myself and sat in eerie luxury: just me and a box of noisy popcorn. For a few hours I immersed myself in Regency England, before emerging into the dystopian world of Covid-19 Level 4 lockdown.

Along with what seemed like most of the 1.5 million population of Auckland, I headed for the crush of the supermarket. Silly me. We'd been warned not to overreact by stockpiling. But in the same way that a budgie hoovers up seed when it gets nervous, we are, at root, just scared animals with no experience of dealing with a global pandemic. And so we shop. And stockpile. We can, at least, do that.

Feeling a bit ridiculous, I took my loot back home to my two boys. I think I was slightly in shock. What if this global situation got worse? What if it spiralled beyond anything any of us could conceive of? For the first week I soaked up the news, but quickly became saturated with this hypervigilance and started to limit what I watched. The boys and I settled into lockdown, New Zealand style.

I am well aware of how lucky we have been. Why the dice tumbles down so unevenly is one of life's biggest mysteries. Our Prime Minister, Jacinda Ardern, had already done a crash course in crisis. She was at the side of the victims' families in the 2019 mosque massacre and also handled the White Island volcanic eruption, in which seventeen people died. All that in the first year of being PM, as well as having her first baby. Her leadership has made all the difference to us. We closed our borders early, imposed lockdown early, and had sufficient medical stocks and hospital beds. Ardern and her government gave clear guidelines which we trusted, and which mitigated the effects of this terrible pandemic.

At first, life under lockdown felt fine, and not so very different from normal. I'm a musician and already work from home with some of my projects. The boys like being at home. And the cat looked at me triumphantly. "Ah!" she seemed to say. "You've finally seen sense! You're going to sit in the sun and listen to the birds!"

Reality soon hit. My performances had ground to a halt, and I needed to earn some money. What if there was no more live music this year? The thought was horrific: music is both my income and my passion. The boys had to adjust, too. One had to cope with schooling on his own, and the other was separated from his girlfriend and unable to work.

But talk about straightening out our priorities! I'm so grateful that we have stayed healthy. Without your health you are nothing: there is no lifestyle to enjoy. And I was so glad to have my two boys safe. After a talk at the beginning, in which we agreed to be kinder to each other, we really bonded. For the first time in ages, my eighteen-year-old relaxed: with no pressure on him, he was able simply to be present in the space that a lockdown day gave him. It was one of his most prolific music-writing periods, and he lay down multiple tracks. My fifteen-year-old is naturally focused and motivated: he did his schoolwork, read, practised the drums, created music and just hung out. I walked and danced (alone, badly and madly), connected with people online who I hadn't talked to for years, recorded my own music tracks and even began reading a book. Miraculous.

All the same, I found lockdown difficult. I started teaching by Zoom, and problems with lag and sound drops made this extremely challenging. For every hour spent teaching, I was doing another of music accompaniments, research, scanning, emailing, checking-in and scheduling. After three weeks I was so tired: teaching like this felt like pushing my head through a screen. It hurt. And my outside-work activities, which normally provided a much-needed change of scene and recharge of batteries, were not available. I had to take some time off my private teaching – but since I don't get paid if I don't work, that hurt too.

Four weeks in, my eighteen-year-old was really struggling and I was finding the whole 24/7 solo parenting thing was wearing thin. My students were tired and stressed and dropping away. Luckily New Zealand moved into Level 3 and my son was able to reconnect with his girlfriend and be with her family. And I could swim in the ocean once more, which was literally the embodiment of freedom: swimming away from the shore with its miserable virus and workload and locked-up crankiness.

I'm so grateful to be living in a country where the tough stuff was handled by clear leadership and we could pretty quickly resume a level of freedom that, even as I write, I know many in the world are still hankering after. I feel very lucky.

Janine's story

I am absolutely terrified of being sick, so when coronavirus hit the headlines at the beginning of the year, I was just relieved it didn't present itself as a vomiting bug.

Little did I know what terrible times lay ahead...

I listened to the news about China going into lockdown and hospitals being erected within a couple of weeks, but since it was all happening thousands of miles away I didn't for a moment imagine that the situation would be mirrored here in the UK.

As a trainee nurse and healthcare assistant in an NHS hospital, I remember the day my phone pinged at work. The text was from the temporary staffing office, asking for staff of all grades to volunteer to work at the local hotel which was about to become an isolation unit for a group of people being repatriated from the Wuhan region. The hospital had agreed to staff this unit for the two week quarantine period and needed volunteers to provide everyday care and act as runners to meet people's needs while they were in isolation. Given the horror stories coming out of China, my immediate thought was that they would struggle to get volunteers, even though they were offering triple pay.

Word soon got round and although some accused The Trust of encouraging staff to sell their souls to the devil, others were already dreaming about what they would spend the extra income on. Whatever people's views, these ex-pats needed looking after, and somebody had to do it.

As time went on, the nation became fixated on the daily Covid bulletins and things began to change at work. Wards were closed to create isolation areas and metal framework appeared in A&E to cordon off an area referred to as the 'Red Zone'. Plastic sheeting with special zipped doors was hung from the framework, and PPE placed outside. It looked like something out of *ET*. DO NOT ENTER signs became part of the fixtures and fittings, and updates were sent to all staff. We were advised that our annual leave might be cancelled at short notice and that some of us would have to be redeployed to specialised areas.

And then we waited. By now, the whole country was in full lockdown and the hospital looked like a ghost town. The corridors were no longer filled with patients' families and friends. Outpatient appointments and elective surgeries were cancelled and, where possible, non-clinical staff were allowed to work from home. A&E, which was normally packed, became scarily quiet. People were too afraid to come through the doors.

It soon became apparent that those who did come into A&E were genuinely sick and needed urgent medical attention. Some left it too late. I remember one lady being rushed off for emergency surgery, who under normal circumstances would have come in sooner. Her operation ended up being far more complicated than it might otherwise have been. She required intensive care admission but had to remain on a general surgical ward because of the numerous Covid patients occupying the ICU beds. She died. Would this have happened if she hadn't been afraid of coming into hospital because of Covid? Would she have survived had there been an ICU bed available? Who knows? Personally, I believe that this pandemic has caused far more deaths throughout the world than statistics will ever show. I'm sure there are many who have died as a consequence of Covid rather than of the virus itself, though these people will never be included in the statistics.

I have been very lucky. My family and I have remained healthy and in some respects have appreciated the slower pace of life that lockdown has brought us. I have continued to work in a job I love, with colleagues I respect and value. My nursing course has been put on hold, but I have a guaranteed place back at university once this is all over.

I hope some good things will come of it. Perhaps we won't take as much for granted. Perhaps we will be more appreciative of the simple things in life, like being able to see our family and friends. Perhaps we will realise how fortunate we are to have access to the NHS. Whatever happens, nobody will ever forget it. I look forward to the time when I sit down and tell my grandchildren all about the 2020 pandemic. My story won't start with the words, "During the war…", but Covid-19 has certainly been the biggest international fight of the twenty-first century so far.

Samantha's story

What do chocolate, hot cross buns and a jigsaw puzzle have in common? Strange as it may sound, they're my night-shift survival tools during the coronavirus pandemic.

I'm not a healthcare worker and can't begin to imagine what their life is like right now. I work for the Foreign Office, and since Covid-19 kicked off we've had millions of British tourists and travellers overseas who've suddenly found themselves in countries in lockdown, with borders and airports closing, and airlines cancelling flights. Families have been divided and tourists stranded, worried about their health and running out of money. I've been part of the London team set up to try and bring them home.

Almost all British Embassies have been part of this effort. In some cases it has involved diplomacy, persuading host governments to give airlines permission to keep flying, or to keep open transit airports so that long-haul flights can make it home. In others it has meant persuading airlines to continue running: we have supplied them with enough passengers to keep them viable. There's been a massive attempt to get home British nationals on cruise ships, which have had particular problems with the virus. And a big part of the effort has been chartering planes to destinations around the world to bring back British tourists who suddenly have no other way of coming home.

In London that has meant working out where the most vulnerable are, obtaining permission to land flights and signing up airlines to work with us to supply these charters. There have been all sorts of hidden logistics: we've found ourselves operating like airlines, having to deal with passenger manifests and advance passenger information (for example, alerting airports so that they have enough wheelchairs available when flights land, or asking for special help from airports to open early or to stay open late).

At the time of writing (early May), we have brought home 30,000 travellers, including passengers on over fifty flights from India alone. We've had hundreds of people working twenty-four hours a day in shifts to make all this happen: some liaising with airlines on commercial routes, some planning and analysing where we needed to send charters and how to do it (for example, how to charter small aircraft to collect tourists from islands across the Philippines), others working on contracts with airlines, and still more working through the logistics of planning on the ground.

Our Embassies around the world have put in the most extraordinary effort. In Nepal, staff, drivers and Gurkhas have driven over four thousand miles to get Brits in remote places to the airport so that they could get on our charter flights. Travellers have been bused across India to the major cities. One woman was driven across India the equivalent distance of Moscow to London just to catch her flight. All this has involved getting permission for our tourists to move around during lockdowns and to cross closed borders.

I haven't been on the front line. I've been working from my dining-room table – overnight – with colleagues who have also been trying to make lockdown and home-working happen. I'm lucky: I have a house with a garden, and kids more-or-less old enough to entertain themselves. Others in the team haven't been so fortunate: some have had to operate from tiny flats on their own or juggle the needs of small children.

I feel lucky that at this time of national crisis I have been able to do something to help. But I couldn't have managed without the chocolate (my midnight snacks), the hot cross buns (my early-morning breakfasts) and the jigsaw puzzle (with which I shared the dining-room table). These small things have kept me sane, because the big thing has been – and still is – too much to take in.

Sharona's story

Many times in the past I have lamented being tied to my often-unsatisfying job, complained about having to maintain an old, crumbling house, stared discontentedly out of the window at the weed-ridden, overgrown garden, or moaned about French bureaucracy. Lockdown changed all that. Never have I been so grateful for the security of my contract, the tranquillity of my garden, the reassuring comfort of my home and the glorious weather that accompanied almost every day. For the first time in my life, I was energised to attack the garden and turn it into a space I could enjoy. The more backbreaking the task, the more pleasure I derived from it: path-building, terrace-laying, the endless monotony of weeding and pulling up roots, knocking the rendering off the walls of outbuildings. The repetition was soothing and meditative.

Like so many people, confronted by the fear of not being able to get hold of the food I needed, I felt the urge to cultivate my own produce. At the start of lockdown, my intention had been to use the time constructively: maybe to do a language course on the internet, and not waste a moment. I took a very different path, one I would never have imagined. Every morning the day began, cup of tea in hand, with a joyful inspection of my seedling 'babies' and their development. Language courses were supplanted by the study of the pollination of courgette plants, the bolting of coriander and the successful cultivation of tomatoes. One day a duck appeared in the pond, waiting patiently for her six ducklings to make their first jump into the water to join her. Hours were spent in observation, researching their behaviour and dietary needs, laying out little plates of oats, corn and berries for them, fearing for the arrival of the neighbour's cat. Five days later, to our dismay, they waddled out of the garden, never to return.

As lockdown eased, so did my energy levels and motivation. My early-evening walks along the riverbank (equipped with the necessary government documentation, allowing me one excursion a day of no further than a kilometre) ground to a halt. As the cars returned to the roads, I no longer heard so distinctly the cuckoo and the woodpecker that had accompanied me on my woodland walks. Although much time was spent pottering in the garden and no online courses were ever completed – or even begun – at least I was able to bring my first tomatoes, courgettes, salads and spring onions to the table and share them proudly with my loved ones.

Many have struggled and suffered deep loss during this time, and I am very much aware of my good fortune, and the stark differences in experience that such privileges bring. Nevertheless, when I look back, I shall feel a sense of nostalgia, surrounded as I was by my family, and with all of us secure, comfortable and in good health.

Hat's story

The dipper told me.

It was perched on a rock, a plump, dark little thing with a short tail and a white throat, singing its heart out in the stream below the reservoir. It seemed to know I was there, but it didn't fly away. Even when I left the frogspawn I'd been inspecting and inched closer to get a better look, it continued its song – a sweet, sad ripple, barely distinguishable from the rushing water.

News of the virus had been gathering pace for days. I'd felt uneasy all weekend, checking the headlines and flicking through the updates on my phone. If I hadn't already sensed the seriousness of what was coming, I sensed it now.

For a long while I just stood there and listened, a captive audience of one, until at last I grew cold and turned back to the path, straining my ears as the dipper's melody receded into the vast melancholy of the late February afternoon.

At the start of May, I returned. By then we were on our way down from the peak of the pandemic and as I walked up the path from the car park, I spotted not one but two dippers, bobbing about in the stream. Above me, the sky was an uninterrupted blue.

In the distance a cuckoo competed for my attention, but I heard only the dippers' watery burble.

Perhaps they were warning me not to be complacent. Perhaps they were telling me that it was all far from over, that we'd only seen the start of things.

I prefer to believe it was a song of hope.

Please join us online:

Facebook: The Little Taboo

Twitter/Instagram: @thelittletaboo

We'd love to see you there!

If you've enjoyed reading this book, you might also be interested in the others in the series:

The Menopause Monologues

The Menopause Monologues II

Thanks

… to Gabriel, for the long country walks, the excellent company and the education into seriously good coffee.

Printed in Great Britain
by Amazon